THE SUPREME COURT IN AMERICAN POLITICS

PROBLEMS IN POLITICAL SCIENCE

under the editorial direction of NEAL RIEMER, *University of Wisconsin–Milwaukee*

WESTERN EUROPE: WHAT PATH TO INTEGRATION?
edited by CAROL EDLER BAUMANN, *University of Wisconsin–Milwaukee*

THE REPRESENTATIVE: TRUSTEE? DELEGATE? PARTISAN? POLITICO?
edited by NEAL RIEMER, *University of Wisconsin–Milwaukee*

FREE SPEECH AND POLITICAL PROTEST
edited by MARVIN SUMMERS, *University of Wisconsin–Milwaukee*

THE AMERICAN POLITICAL EXPERIENCE: WHAT IS THE KEY?
edited by EDWARD HANDLER, *Babson Institute*

THE CENTRAL INTELLIGENCE AGENCY: PROBLEMS OF SECRECY IN A DEMOCRACY
edited by YOUNG HUM KIM, *California Western University–USIU*

LIBERALIZATION IN THE USSR: FACADE OR REALITY?
edited by D. RICHARD LITTLE, *Northern Illinois University*

THE BLACK REVOLT AND DEMOCRATIC POLITICS
edited by SONDRA SILVERMAN, *City University of New York*

KARL MARX: SCIENTIST? REVOLUTIONARY? HUMANIST?
edited by V. STANLEY VARDYS, *University of Oklahoma*

JEAN-JACQUES ROUSSEAU: AUTHORITARIAN LIBERTARIAN?
edited by GUY H. DODGE, *Brown University*

THE SUPREME COURT IN AMERICAN POLITICS: JUDICIAL ACTIVISM VS. JUDICIAL RESTRAINT
edited by DAVID F. FORTE, *Skidmore College*

THE SUPREME COURT IN
AMERICAN POLITICS

Judicial Activism vs. Judicial Restraint

EDITED AND WITH AN INTRODUCTION BY

David F. Forte

SKIDMORE COLLEGE

D. C. HEATH AND COMPANY
Lexington, Massachusetts   Toronto   London

FOR NICOLE

CONTENTS

V. THE NON-POLITICAL V. THE POLITICAL COURT

VI. FACING THE REALITY OF A POLITICAL COURT: A CRITICAL ANALYSIS

THE CLASH OF ISSUES

THE CAPABILITIES OF THE JUDICIARY
   Given is insulation, and the inevitably episodic nature of its approach to
   most problems, the Court is not the suitable agency to make administrative decisions, not the agency to *run* anything.
                                                —ALEXANDER M. BICKEL

   Surely it is not the place of the Court to abdicate this role because it
   thinks someone else could play it better, any more than it is the place of
   the President to stop appointing judges because he thinks it would be
   wise for them to be elected.
                                                —CHARLES L. BLACK, JR.

THE SUPREME COURT AND THE DEMOCRATIC PROCESS
   And so, from first to last, Felix Frankfurter was wary of judicial efforts
   to impose justice on the people—to force upon them "better" government
   than they were able at the moment to give themselves. It was his deepest
   conviction that no five men, or nine, are wise enough or good enough to
   wield such power over an entire nation. Morris R. Cohen put it bluntly:
   If judges are to govern, they ought to be elected.
                                                —WALLACE MENDELSON

   By protecting the integrity and unobstructed operation of the process by
   which majorities are formed, judicial review becomes a surrogate for
   revolution, contributing positively to government resting on consent.

                                                —ALPHEUS T. MASON

JUDICIAL FAVORITISM
   . . . The Court exhibits the characteristics of other agencies of government. It is subject to lobbying by a wide range of groups, some of whom
   find it essential, others merely a supplementary, source of representation. It will, on occasion, give marginal assistance to nearly any interest.
   But if it wishes to act effectively in the long run, the Court must reserve
   its major efforts for its particular clientele.
                                                —MARTIN SHAPIRO

   . . . It certainly does not accord with the underlying presuppositions of
   popular government to vest in a chamber, unaccountable to anyone but
   itself, the power to suppress social experiments which it does not approve.

                                                —LEARNED HAND

I. INTRODUCTION

WHAT is the role of the Supreme Court in the American system of government? Despite its catechismic tone, this question has been agitating the country since the Constitutional Convention of 1787. The debate has intensified of late, for in recent years the Supreme Court has been the initiator of far-reaching changes in our political system. Today, as has been the case for decades, the debate centers on whether the Court in its actions should be "active" or "restrained." Since discussion of both the Warren Court and the Burger Court is directed to this question, it is desirable that the student of the Court be familiar with arguments from both sides. This book of readings is intended to be such a discussion of the problem.

As the controversy over the Court has sharpened year by year, it has become clear that the question goes beyond the desirability of those political and social changes wrought by the Court. It concerns the very definition of the constitutional system, the relation of the Court to it, and whether the Court is a proper agent for significant change in the polity. To understand the Court we cannot look at it "in the void" as it were. Rather, a proper perspective can be obtained only by observing the Court in relation to the other parts of the system, to Congress, the President, the states, the lower courts, interest groups, public opinion, and so on. Indeed, most analysts of Supreme Court behavior, whether of the activist or restrained school, have viewed the Court in these terms. It is only in this fashion that we can confront the central issue: what has been, is, and ought to be, the proper role of the Supreme Court in a democratic, constitutional, and federal America?

The student of the Supreme Court must resolve in his mind far more than whether the activist justices are more correct than the restrained justices. He has first to determine just what is meant by activism and by restraint. This is no easy task, for the very definitions of judicial activism and judicial restraint, as well as their evaluation, depend on one's conception of the American political system. Indeed, much of today's disagreement over the Court lies not in the specific issue at hand, but in the antagonists' unspoken assumptions of what is, in fact, the American political system. That question must be solved first, before we can focus clearly on the Court. Different problems arise when we view the United States political system in different contexts. The following are some brief descriptions of the American political structure and what sort of role for the Supreme Court they entail.

To begin, let us examine the classic constitutional model of checks and balances to see what sort of analysis of judicial activity that model suggests. As we know, the prime objective of this model was defined as preventing "tyranny." This was to be accomplished by keeping one branch from acquiring inordinate power over the other two branches and, for that matter, over the states as well. On the federal level, each of the branches had the power to "check" the other branches. Each was given "partial agency" in the affairs of the other branches so that each branch became accountable for its actions. When a President submits a legislative program or vetoes a bill, he is participating in the legislative process. When Congress oversees the bureaucracy, it has a say in executive dealings. Likewise, though the President's power to appoint justices, and the Congress' right to establish the appellate jurisdiction of the Supreme Court, both the President and Congress participate in the judicial process. Partial agency in the affairs of coordinate branches was built into the constitutional system from the start. However, there is an argument which asserts that the involvement of one branch in the affairs of another may become too extensive. There are constitutional and practical limitations on

1

the degree of participation of one branch in the activities of another. Similarly, the constitutional structure which left a great many powers in the hands of the states may also be endangered through the expansion of federal power.

The key point made in this scheme is that partial agency, originally designed as a tool of limitation, has of late become instead a tool of expansion of power. In this situation, the only method of avoiding the undue acquisition of power is for a branch to eschew voluntarily the enlargement of its own power. This is called the exercise of self-restraint. Each branch should be concerned with the extent of its own power, as well as that of other branches. For example, if a President wishes to be free of the constitutional proviso that the Senate approve treaties, he will make an "executive agreement" instead. The difference between a treaty and executive agreement has yet to be clearly defined. It is the President's choice whether to follow the literal constitutional procedure. From this model, one can see the outlines of one of the more prominent arguments for self-restraint by the Supreme Court. It holds that the Court has gone too far afield and should apply the constitutional limitations of its role to itself. This school argues that the Court itself has been acting unconstitutionally. Many of the selections that follow are partially or wholly based on this point of view. See the articles by Hand, Mendelson, and Harlan.

It should be noted that this conception of the role of the Supreme Court depends on two rather contentious propositions: (1) that the Court must exercise self-restraint because the attempts of the other branches at checking the Court have rarely been applied with effect; and (2) that the classic constitutional model is relevant to American politics today.

The first proposition is arguable. Formal checks on the Court have not been very frequent. Impeachment of a Supreme Court justice was attempted but once, and he was not convicted. The denial of appellate jurisdiction by Congress occurred only once, during the reconstruction period of American history. There have been three occasions when a constitutional amendment was passed to overturn a Supreme Court decision. There have been only three, perhaps four, changes of judicial policy brought about explicitly by new appointments to the bench. In recent years the technique of the appointment or non-appointment of justices has figured large in the attempt of coordinate branches of the federal government to influence the Court. Despite the rhetoric about "conflict of interest," the controversies surrounding Fortas, Haynesworth, Carswell, and Douglas were really contests over judicial policy. Nonetheless, even where a President succeeds in having his nominees approved by the Senate, the desired change in Court direction often does not come about. The appointments made by President Nixon may have changed Court decisions in the field of persons accused of crimes, but the Nixon administration received little comfort in the decisions on desegregation. In sum, as in the past, new appointments to the bench have only occasionally changed judicial policy in any dramatic fashion. The advocates of restraint hold that these checks have mattered little in comparison to the number of instances when the Court has overstepped its proper bounds. They point to the Warren Court which, despite its controversial and questionable activism, was in little danger of being checked. In reality, they say, there is no formal governmental agent external to the Court which limits it in any substantial way. Therefore, it is up to the Court to police its own actions.

The second proposition, that the classic constitutional model is an accurate description of American government today, is much more severely contested. During the past decade many, if not most, political scientists have thought this institutional model misleading and outdated. They see the American political process more as a dynamic system of group conflict. The process is regarded not as one of separation of powers, but as "separate institutions sharing power." A neat division of responsibility is not the way politics works. The premise on which the advocates of restraint based their views is denied. The selection by Shapiro illustrates this. On the other hand, the recent conflict between the executive and Congress over the Vietnam war and over domestic issues demonstrates anew to many political scientists how vibrant the institution of the separation of powers continues to be.

However, even if we grant the advocate of restraint his argument so far, and accept this description of the classic constitutional model as true, we shall find that his problems have just begun. Once the advocate of restraint accepts the responsibilties of judicial review in checking the other departments of government, and in umpiring the federal system, he has to face the question of when judicial review is an acceptable activity, and when it is an undesirable interference. No consistent criterion has yet been followed.

A common argument purportedly used in favor of the activists is one which uses the classic constitutional model as outlined above, but which claims that the greatest check on the Court is the informal one of public opinion, and not the formal constitutional checks. The Court, in this view, does not have to worry about its proper "sphere" or activity vis-à-vis the other branches of government. It need only keep one eye cocked on public opinion which will enforce clear limitations on any attempt at overextending judicial power. This argument is still very common in university courses on constitutional law, but most modern defenders of an activist court avoid it, for it has weaknesses. A look at historical evidence would throw some doubt on whether public opinion, by itself, ever checked the Court's actions. It would seem that it did so only when a coordinate branch of government took up the same cause. In addition, as we saw above, such attacks on the Court by the coordinate branches have only been successful infrequently, even if we include

such unfulfilled threats as Roosevelt's Court-packing plan. The "informal" check of public opinion generally has no effect unless it is translated into one of the more "formal" constitutional checks. And as the advocates of restraint like to point out, even that is not much to count on. The one exception whereby the public does check the Court involves a recent practice of non-compliance especially in the areas of school prayers and desegregation. But this fact is used not by the activists, but by the restraintists who argue that the Court has overstepped the bounds of credible authority. See the argument made by Kurland.

A variation of this view is that public opinion has not had to check the Court often because the Court has consistently and accurately reflected the desires of the people. The Court avoids a conflict with the popular will by making decisions already in harmony with it. Public opinion, then, positively guides the Court. This position is based upon a majoritarian populist view of American democracy. It assumes that people's opinions are generally unified, clearly articulated, and are a conscious expression of the will of the majority. Despite its undemocratic structure, the Court acts according to the will of the people. This view, too, is often broached in courses on constitutional law. "The Court follows the election returns" is the phrase often heard. But the modern activist does not care for this defense of his position. For one thing, it assumes certain political structures which the activist of today does not think accurate. Most observers nowadays think that the American political base is pluralistic, not majoritarian or populistic. It is thought that few issues excite the majority of people, that, in fact, America is made up of a series of overlapping minority groups. In addition, in regard to the decisions of the Warren Court, the evidence seems to contradict the formulative role of public opinion. For the most part, popular views are rarely so articulate that a clear majoritarian desire can be ascertained. The great social decisions of the Warren Court in the fields of desegregation, reapportionment, rights of persons accused of crimes, school prayers, fringe group activities, cannot be said to have been the result of any public clamor. The Court listened to certain minority groups: blacks, law professors, newspaper editorial writers, but grass-roots public opinion was not evident These decisions either brought the issues to the general public's consciousness for the first time, or they actually went against public opinion. It does not seem useful to think of the Supreme Court's decisions as following majoritarian public opinion. If anything, it presages it.

Those in favor of a restrained role for the Court often use the minority group basis of American politics not only to counter those who rely on public opinion, but also to further their own view of the Court. The American polity is made up of disparate groups. The Supreme Court is responsible to very few of them—electorally to none. Furthermore, the nature of the judicial process in our country lies in the adversary system. Very often the Court is faced with an either/or choice with a narrow range of facts and variables before it. The Court simply is not structured to adjust and compromise the myriad group demands that other "more democratic" branches are able to. The Court simply lacks the capacity of successfully meeting political issues. The President and Congress have a greater capacity. This advocacy of a restrained judicial role is based more on the lack of capacity of the Court to deal with problems, rather than on its "constitutional" role. See the selection by Bickel. The activists dispute this view of course, because they think it does not go far enough. There are some groups, especially the unorganized, which do not have access to the "democratic" centers of power. Why should not the Court be their spokesman? See the article by Mason for this view.

On his part, the activist does much better when he shifts the basis of discussion. A common argument of the activists is that the Constitution is not primarily the classic model of divided powers, but that it is first of all a charter of rights. "The Bill of Rights is the heart of any constitution," as Chief Justice Earl Warren put it. This is an attractive thesis in theory, but it runs into problems when viewed historically. The point is that even those of the founding fathers who supported a bill of rights held that tyranny was prevented by the actual division of governmental powers, not by mere general guarantees. Furthermore, even if one accepts the contrary view, that the Bill of Rights is central in the Constitution, one finds that the application of this rule is often contractory. This attitude holds that the Court ought to be active in furthering individual rights, and it can either support or reject the use of certain governmental powers, depending on how the individual fares. Yet, it is curious that in the two recent eras of judicial activism—the laissez-faire Court of the 1920's and 1930's, and the Warren Court of the 1950's and 1960's—individual rights were defined quite differently. The laissez-faire Court was concerned with individual and group economic rights, and had only a slight regard for political rights. On the other hand, the Warren Court was completely involved in individual and group political rights, and gave short shrift to any argument concerning economic rights. Some observers find the distinction eminently reasonable. Others hold that it is an unjustifiable contradiction.

The analyses outlined so far are only a few of those offered to explain the differences between judicial activism and judicial restraint. There are many more. For example, there is the classic argument that the two sides to the controversy merely reflect the historical differences between a broad construction of the Constitution (the Hamiltonian view) and a narrow one (the Jeffersonian view). One group will interpret the delegation of governmental powers broadly (and, consequently, the Bill of Rights narrowly), while the other group construes the governmental powers strictly (and the Bill of Rights broadly). There is a connection here with the "Charter of Rights" theory of the Constitution. As a matter of fact, a contemporary justification for judicial activism is that the Constitution contains "preferred freedoms," that the Bill of Rights is somehow worth more than the other sections of the Constitution. But looking more closely at this classic theory of broad versus narrow construction, it is difficult to see which group corresponds to the activists and which group to the advocates of restraint. Chief Justice John Marshall made brilliant use of broad construction to aid the powers of government, and he is often categorized as an activist. On the other hand, the activist laissez-faire Court continuously construed governmental power strictly. Moreover, some Courts mix strict and broad construction. For example, the Warren Court strictly construed the state and national power to apportion legislative districts, but it broadly construed congressional power to enforce integration at the most local level.

Another view holds that activist justices are in favor of a more nationalist state while the restrained justices give more room to the powers of the states. In today's Court, this debate is carried on in terms of whether the due process clause of the 14th Amendment incorporates all, some, or none of the Bill of Rights and applies them against the states. But again, this tool is difficult to apply to the laissez-faire Court, because in many instances, the Court went to great lengths to limit the federal government's interstate commerce power. (The laissez-faire Court also used the due process clause of the 14th Amendment to limit what it regarded as undesirable state social legislation, but never in order to expand the federal government's power in the area.)

It is no longer held that activists are political liberals and restraintists of political conservatives. The laissez-faire Court of Sutherland et al. were activist conservatives, while Frankfurter was a restrained liberal. Nevertheless, there is one current school which still relates activism/restraint to policy attitudes. It states that the justices of the Supreme Court are active when they happen to oppose a policy championed by Congress or the Executive and, concomitantly, that they are restrained when they agree with the policy espoused by the other two branches. See the article by Schubert. This view suggests that restrained justices are really only activist wolves in sheep's clothing, and that these justices will shed their disguise if the other branches embark upon an undesired policy. No doubt some justices fit this description. Some who were restrained in the 1930's became activists in the 1940's and 1950's. But not all justices have a thorough-going policy bias. Justices Felix Frankfurter and John Marshall Harlan, II, for instance, seem to pursue a consistently conservative idea of the role of the judiciary. Furthermore, certain activist justices cannot be defined merely by their opposition to Congressional or Executive policy. Some also initiate new policies in certain fields. The requirement of the one-man one-vote standard in state and Congressional apportionment schemes might be one such example. Nevertheless, a policy bias on the part of certain justices is objected to strongly by advocates of judicial restraint. A more "neutral" standard of judging is called for. See the article by Wechsler and the replies by Miller and Howell for an elaboration of this discussion.

There is another mode of analysis which suggests that the advocates of restraint are interested in preserving the structure of the American political system, while the activists are more concerned with immediate social reform. This is a variation of the view that the former see the Constitution as a formula for dividing power and the latter see it as a charter of rights. If we compare the opinions of Chief Justice Warren with those of Justice Harlan, this point of view makes some sense. The debate is very often phrased in terms of structure versus rights. But if we try to apply this formula to earlier courts, it runs into trouble. Chief Justice Marshall, an activist, was more interested in structure. The laissez-faire Court was interested in furthering certain social values, certain rights. But on the other hand, it was also exceedingly interested in the structure of the political system. It consistently sought to gains its ends through an analysis of division of powers, through defining the structure of the governing institutions. It was wary of the delegation of power. This sort of attitude was almost absent in the Warren Court.

Finally, there is a most interesting viewpoint which is gaining wide currency nowadays. This concept rejects the classical constitutional model as being unreal, and it also regards such distinctions as broad and narrow construction as irrelevant. It suggests that there are a myriad of power centers in the government, from the Interstate Commerce Commission to the Senate Judiciary Committee to the Office of Economic Opportunity to the Supreme Court, all of which convert various supports and demands into both normative and distributive decisions. There is no neat delineation of responsibility and competence between three separate branches. Instead there are these institutional centers of power within which the pluralistic group competition of the American polity takes place. The Supreme Court is one of these active policy-making centers and it should not be afraid of accepting this role.

The proponents of this viewpoint do not accept the charge that this places an "undemocratic" institution at an unfair advantage over the more "democratic" institutions and the groups they represent. On the contrary, they argue that certain groups are prevented by the institutional structure of the government from gaining access to the centers of power within the Executive, the Congress, or the states. Consequently, if the Court becomes an active champion of these groups, it actually completes the democratic process by incorporating all groups within the decision-making arena.

Needless to say, this viewpoint also engenders its own problems. Because of the limitations of the adversary process, the Court may not be capable of adjusting one group's claims to the claims of others and of society in general. In any given case, the Court has

very few groups before it, and is given a very narrow range of choices. In other arenas of government, groups in competition find that some degree of cooperation and compromise is necessary. This need not be the case in the judicial process. The Court's intrusion into the political realm of competing groups' demands may actually throw the system into an imbalance, for certain favored groups will receive an unfair advantage. Also, there is a myth necessary to the functioning of a liberal democracy. It is that the rules and procedures (that is, the law) under which the groups compete should be universal and neutral. The law, therefore, keeps group conflict within certain bounds. If the "guardian" of the law turns it into the parochial benefit of a particular group, then the authority of the law may be denied by the other groups. The Court may therefore help engender a crisis in political legitimacy.

These are some of the approaches lurking behind the debate over the Court today. Although some writers think that the Court's concern with activism and restraint mislead it as to its proper role (see the article by Shapiro), and others find it an inadequate means of analyzing Court behavior (see the selection by Schubert), nonetheless, it is clear that to the justices themselves the concepts of judicial activism and judicial restraint are centrally relevant to the way they decide many of the controversies brought before them. Their opinions reflect this explicitly.

Finally, even if we do make our analysis of the Court in these terms, it must not be supposed that self-restraint and activism in judicial behavior are two mutually exclusive alternatives. On the contrary, they are the two poles of a wide purview of possible judicial behavior. There has never been a Court or a justice who was, in all actions, totally committed to self-restraint, nor was there one absolutely engaged in activism. The American political system makes a complete commitment to either pole untenable. We can try, however, to determine toward what end of the restraint-activism pole the Court of any one period tends to lean. For instance, it is generally held that the Warren Court was close to the pole of activism, while the previous Vinson Court was, on balance, nearer to the pole of restraint. The Burger Court seems to be wavering somewhere in between its two predecessors. Yet if we ask any student of the Court why the Warren Court was activist or, more importantly, whether it ought to have been activist, we are once again thrown back upon various models of our political system which shape our evaluation of a Court's behavior. This book contains readings which will elaborate the various positions as outlined above. It will serve, it is to be hoped, to expand the student's awareness of the American political system and provide him with a deeper understanding of one of its unique institutions.

II. TWO PERSPECTIVES ON JUDICIAL REVIEW

A Structural Interpretation

John P. Roche

JUDICIAL SELF-RESTRAINT

John P. Roche has combined academic, governmental, and political interests in his career. He is now the Morris Hillquit professor of politics and history at Brandeis University, and was formerly dean of the faculty there. He has been national chairman for the Americans for Democratic Action, and was a special consultant to President Johnson. His publications include *Shadow and Substance* (1964), *The Quest for the Dream* (1963), *Courts and Rights,* second edition (1966), and *The Writings of John Marshall* (1966). He also edited, with L. W. Levy, *The Judiciary: Documents in American Government* (1964).

. . . EVERYWHERE one turns in the United States, he finds institutionalized attempts to narrow the political sector and to substitute allegedly "independent" and "impartial" bodies for elected decision-makers. The so-called "independent regulatory commissions" are a classic example of this tendency in the area of administration, but unquestionably the greatest hopes for injecting pure Truth-serum into the body politic have been traditionally reserved for the federal judiciary, and particularly for the Supreme Court. The rationale for this viewpoint is simple: "The people must be protected from themselves, and no institution is better fitted for the role of chaperon than the federal judiciary, dedicated as it is to the supremacy of the rule of law."

Patently central to this function of social chaperonage is the right of the judiciary to review legislative and executive actions and nullify those measures which derogate from eternal principles of truth and justice as incarnated in the Constitution. Some authorities, enraged at what the Supreme Court has found the Constitution to mean, have essayed to demonstrate that the Framers did not intend the Court to exercise this function, to have, as they put it, "the last word." I find no merit in this contention; indeed, it seems to me undeniable not only that the authors of the Constitution intended to create a federal government, but also that they assumed *sub silentio* that the Supreme Court would have the power to review both national and state legislation.

However, since the intention of the Framers is essentially irrelevant except to antiquarians and polemicists, it is unnecessary to examine further the matter of origins. The fact is that the United States Supreme Court, and the inferior federal courts under the oversight of the high Court, have enormous policy-making functions. Unlike their British and French counterparts, federal judges are not merely technicians who live in the shadow of a supreme legislature, but are

Source: "Judicial Self-Restraint," *American Political Science Review*, Vol. XLIX, No. 3 (September, 1955), pp. 762–772.

fully equipped to intervene in the process of political decision-making. In theory, they are limited by the Constitution and the jurisdiction it confers, but, in practice, it would be a clumsy judge indeed who could not, by a little skillful exegesis, adapt the Constitution to a necessary end. This statement is in no sense intended as a condemnation; on the contrary, it has been this perpetual reinvigoration by reinterpretation, in which the legislature and the executive as well as the courts play a part, that has given the Constitution its survival power. Applying a Constitution which contains at key points inspired ambiguity, the courts have been able to pour the new wine in the old bottle. Note that the point at issue is not the legitimacy or wisdom of judicial legislation; it is simply the enormous scope that this prerogative gives to judges to substitute their views for those of past generations, or, more controversially, for those of a contemporary Congress and President.

Thus it is naive to assert that the Supreme Court is limited by the Constitution, and we must turn elsewhere for the sources of judicial restraint. The great power exercised by the Court has carried with it great risks, so it is not surprising that American political history has been sprinkled with demands that the judiciary be emasculated. The really startling thing is that, with the notable exception of the McCardle incident in 1869, the Supreme Court has emerged intact from each of these encounters. Despite the plenary power that Congress, under Article III of the Constitution, can exercise over the appellate jurisdiction of the high Court, the national legislature has never taken sustained and effective action against its House of Lords. It is beyond the purview of this analysis to examine the reasons for congressional inaction, suffice it here to say that the most significant form of judicial limitation has remained self-limitation. This is not to suggest that such a development as statutory codification has not cut down the area of interpretive discretion, for it obviously has. It is rather to maintain that when the justices have held back from assaults on legislative or executive actions, they have done so on the basis of self-established rationalizations such as Justice Brandeis' famous "Ashwander rules.". . .

TECHNIQUES OF JUDICIAL SELF-RESTRAINT

The major techniques of judicial self-restraint appear to fall under the two familiar rubrics: procedural and substantive. Under the former fall the various techniques by which the Court can avoid coming to grips with substantive issues, while under the latter would fall those methods by which the Court, in a substantive holding, finds that the matter at issue in the litigation is not properly one for judicial settlement. Let us examine these two categories in some detail.

Procedural Self-Restraint.

Since the passage of the Judiciary Act of 1925, the Supreme Court has had almost complete control over its business. United States Supreme Court *Rule 38*, which governs the certiorari policy, states (#5) that discretionary review will be granted only "where there are special and important reasons therefor." Professor Fowler Harper has suggested in a series of detailed and persuasive articles on the application of this discretion that the Court has used it in such a fashion as to duck certain significant but controversial problems. . . .

Other related procedural techniques are applicable in some situations. Simple delay can be employed, perhaps in the spirit of the Croatian proverb that "delay is the handmaiden of justice." The case of *Duncan* v. *Kahanamoku*, contesting the validity of military trials of civilians in Hawaii during the war, is a good instance of the judicial stall: Duncan was locked up in August, 1942, and only succeeded in bringing *habeas corpus* action in the District Court in April, 1944. In November,

1944, the Ninth Circuit affirmed the denial of the writ, and Duncan immediately applied to the Supreme Court for certiorari—which was granted in February, 1945. The Supreme Court studied the case carefully while the war ended, and then in February, 1946, determined that Duncan had been improperly convicted. The Japanese-Americans, attempting to get a judicial ruling on the validity of their detainment in relocation centers, met with the same Kafkaesque treatment. However, the technique of procedural self-restraint is founded on the essentially simple gadget of refusing jurisdiction, or of procrastinating the acceptance of jurisdiction, and need not concern us further here.

Substantive Self-Restraint.

Once a case has come before the Court on its merits, the justices are forced to give some explanation for whatever action they may take. Here self-restraint can take many forms, notably, the doctrine of political questions, the operation of judicial parsimony, and —particularly with respect to the actions of administrative officers or agencies—the theory of judicial inexpertise.

The doctrine of political questions is too familiar to require much elaboration here. Suffice it to say that if the Court feels that a question before it, e.g., the legitimacy of a state government, the validity of a legislative apportionment, or the correctness of executive action in the field of foreign relations, is one that is not properly amenable to judicial settlement, it will refer the plaintiff to the "political" organs of government for any possible relief. The extent to which this doctrine is applied seems to be a direct coefficient of judicial egotism, for the definition of a political question can be expanded or contracted in accordian-like fashion to meet the exigencies of the times. A juridical definition of the term is impossible, for at root the logic that supports it is circular: political questions are matters not soluble by the judicial process; matters not soluble by the judicial process are political questions. As an early dictionary explained,

violins are small cellos, and cellos are large violins. . . .

Judicial parsimony is another major technique of substantive self-restraint. In what is essentially a legal application of Occam's razor, the Court has held that it will not apply any more principles to the settlement of a case than are absolutely necessary, e.g., it will not discuss the constitutionality of a law if it can settle the instant case by statutory construction. Furthermore, if an action is found to rest on erroneous statutory construction, the review terminates at that point: the Court will not go on to discuss whether the statute, properly construed, would be constitutional. A variant form of this doctrine, and a most important one, employs the "case or controversy" approach, to wit, the Court, admitting the importance of the issue, inquires as to whether the litigant actually has standing to bring the matter up.

But while on the surface this technique of limitation appears to be quasi-automatic in operation, such is not always the case. For example, the Court held in the United Public Workers and the Alaskan cannery workers cases that the plaintiffs could not get adjudication until the laws they challenged had been employed against them; it also agreed to review the constitutionality of the New York Teacher Loyalty statute *before* anyone had been injured by its operations. Similarly, the Court for years held that a state government had no standing to intervene *parens patriae* on behalf of the interests of its citizens, but changed its mind in 1945 to permit Georgia to bring action under the antitrust laws against twenty railroads.

A classic use of parsimony to escape from a dangerous situation occurred in connection with the evacuation of the Nisei from the West Coast in 1942. Gordon Hirabayashi, in an attempt to test the validity of the regulations clamped on the American-Japanese by the military, violated the curfew and refused to report to an evacuation center. He was convicted on both counts by the district court and sentenced to three months for each offense, the sentences to run *concurrently*. When the case came before the Supreme Court, the justices sustained his conviction for violating the *curfew*, but refused to examine the validity of the evacuation order on the ground that it would not make any difference to Harabayashi anyway; he was in for ninety days no matter what the Court did with evacuation.

A third method of utilizing substantive self-restraint is particularly useful in connection with the activities of executive departments or regulatory agencies, both state and federal. I have entitled it the doctrine of judicial *inexpertise*, for it is founded on the unwillingness of the Court to revise the findings of experts. The earmarks of this form of restraint are great deference to the holdings of the expert agency usually coupled with such a statement as "It is not for the federal courts to supplant the [Texas Railroad] Commission's judgment even in the face of convincing proof that a different result would have been better.". . .

In short, with respect to expert agencies, the Court is equipped with both offensive and defensive gambits. If it chooses to intervene, one set of precedents is brought out, while if it decides to hold back, another set of equal validity is invoked. Perhaps the best summary of this point was made by Justice Harlan in 1910, when he stated bluntly that "the Courts have rarely, if ever, felt themselves so restrained by technical rules that they could not find some remedy, consistent with the law, for acts . . . that violated natural justice or were hostile to the fundamental principles devised for the protection of the essential rights of property.". . .

The power of the Supreme Court to invade the decision-making arena, I submit, is a consequence of that fragmentation of political power which is normal in the United States. No cohesive majority, such as normally exists in Britain, would permit a politically irresponsible judiciary to usurp decision-making functions, but, for complex social and institutional reasons, there are few issues in the United States on which

cohesive majorities exist. The guerrilla warfare which usually rages between Congress and the President, as well as the internal civil wars which are endemic in both the legislature and the administration, give the judiciary considerable room for maneuver. If, for example, the Court strikes down a controversial decision of the Federal Power Commission, it will be supported by a substantial bloc of congressmen; if it supports the FPC's decision, it will also receive considerable congressional support. But the important point is that *either* way it decides the case, there is no possibility that Congress will exact any vengeance on the Court for its action. A disciplined majority would be necessary to clip the judicial wings, and such a majority does not exist on this issue.

On the other hand, when monolithic majorities do exist on issues, the Court is likely to resort to judicial self-restraint. A good case here is the current tidal wave of anti-communist legislation and administrative action, the latter particularly with regard to aliens, which the Court has treated most gingerly. About the only issues on which there can be found cohesive majorities are those relating to national defense, and the Court has, as Clinton Rossiter demonstrated in an incisive analysis, traditionally avoided problems arising in this area irrespective of their constitutional merits. Like the slave who accompanied a Roman consul on his triumph whispering "You too are mortal," the shade of Thad Stevens haunts the Supreme Court chamber to remind the justices what an angry Congress can do. . . .

In short, judicial self-restraint and judicial power seem to be opposite sides of the same coin: it has been by judicious application of the former that the latter has been maintained. A tradition beginning with Marshall's *coup* in *Marbury v. Madison* and running through *Mississippi v. Johnson* and *Ex Parte Vallandigham* to *Dennis v. United States* suggests that the Court's power has been maintained by a wise refusal to employ it in unequal combat.

A Functional Intrepretation

Glendon Schubert

JUDICIAL POLICY-MAKING

Glendon Schubert is a leading authority on the systematic and behavioral approach to the judiciary. Currently William Rand Kenan, Jr. professor of political science at the University of North Carolina, his books include the following titles: *The Judicial Mind* (1965), *Constitutional Politics* (1960), *The Public Interest* (1960), *Judicial Behavior* (1964), and *Quantitative Analysis of Judicial Behavior* (1959). He is also the editor of *Reapportionment* (1965) and *Judicial Decision-Making* (1959).

FOR an understanding of research in judicial decision-making, three theoretical approaches are important: traditional, conventional, and behavioral. . . .

In presenting these three approaches to the study of judicial decision-making, we wish to underscore that, in practice, it is not a matter of the traditional having been displaced by the conventional nor the latter by the behavioral. They are by no means mutually exclusive alternatives, and all three approaches coexist today in research, writing, and teaching related to the American judiciary. In many areas of the general field of study, the only knowledge we have is that which has been accumulated by scholars following the traditional or conventional approaches, and both of these continue to attract the interest and support of many more students of the judiciary than does the behavioral approach. Moreover, judicial behavioralists also investigate both "law" and "groups"—law as a set of normative propositions that give preference to particular patterns of values, and groups as the collectivities of individuals who are associated together for decision-making purposes. . . .

THE TRADITIONAL APPROACH

The fundamental postulates of the analytical theory of law proposed by the nineteenth-century Englishman, John Austin, are that positive law is what *is*, not what ought to be; that positive (or written) law represents the will of the sovereign; and that therefore positive law is the sovereign's command which must be enforced by executive officials and judges. American legal writers found it easy to substitute a "popular sovereign" for the king of England and notions of the "public will" for the command of the sovereign. The relevant policy-making model is the simplistic one to which we have made earlier reference: the people elect legislators who make laws that it is the duty of judges to enforce in their decisions. . . .

The proponents of sociological jurisprudence turned their attention to the source of the norms that provided the policy content of the decisions of appellate courts, but none of them ever attempted to operationalize the question of the relationship between the needs and demands of "society" and the choice of the individual judge. Roscoe Pound and others proposed that the ultimate source of such norms must be the ideals of natural law; Hans Kelsen avoided the problem by leaving the selection of norms up to the "free discretion" of each judge. The legal realists, or proponents of "experimental jurisprudence," attempted to shift attention away from appellate courts to the decision-making of trial courts. Their preoccupation was with a forthright empiricism that rarely was guided by any systematic theoretical formulations; they conceived their job to be to "get at the facts" of what judges did in decision-making. As a consequence, they produced many studies reporting the facts (as they perceived them) about what courts were doing, and this was no doubt a needed supplement to the logic-chopping of the analytical positivists and the norm-study of the sociological jurists. But the realists did not produce a systematic theory of judicial decision-making roles.

At the present time, these three influences coexist like a crazy quilt in most writing and discussion by lawyers, although the analytical predominates among the practicing bar, the sociological among judges, and the realist among law professors. . . .

The other major component of the traditional theory of judicial decision-making is the historical approach. The assumption underlying this approach is that by examining the ways in which previous occupants have acted in roles similar to those of incumbents, we shall better understand the behavior of judges today. . . .

THE CONVENTIONAL APPROACH

Until the end of World War II, the traditional approach completely dominated studies of the judiciary by political scientists, and it still is the dominant approach in the law schools. Among most political scientists, however, the traditional approach has now largely been superseded as the central focus of inquiry by what is essentially a political sociology of the judicial process. This new orthodoxy is usually called the "political process" approach, and it clearly has become a conventional approach, the one most widely accepted by most political scientists. . . .

The basic assumption of the political process ("political jurisprudence") approach is that judges are policy-makers, just like Presidents and congressmen and many administrators. Therefore, the appropriate subject to be studied in investigating the decision-making of courts is not law but the politics of the judiciary. Law, of course, is not ignored; but it is regarded as the policy output of constitutional conventions, legislatures, Presidents, courts, and administrative agencies rather than as some mystical essence. This concept contrasts sharply with that of traditional theory, which characteristically defines law as a "seamless web," a body of logically interrelated norms that somehow is greater than the sum of its component parts. Moreover, the traditional theory denies that judges make law; instead, they "find" or "discover" it, through an expertise that is a product of their legal training and official status. Political process theory assumes that judges do make law but that their function in so doing is primarily a catalytic one.

The fundamental unit upon which political process theory builds is the social group, and politics can be completely described in terms of interaction among groups. . . .

Groups compete with each other while pursuing their interests, and they attempt to maximize their influence upon decision-makers who can make or maintain policies that will favor the groups. Consequently, there is an interplay of what usually are called "pressures" but sometimes are denominated as "forces." It should be clear that given this Newtonian model, the result must be that decisions of public officials are vectors which are the direct product of the combination of forces brought to bear upon the decision-maker. The result, therefore, is a conception of judicial decision-making that is just as mechanical as John Austin's hierarchies of sovereign power, but the political process theorists require much more elaborate engines to do their work. The residual category of traditional theory, *the law*, has been re-placed by the residual category of the process theory, *the group*. Both tend to ignore the psychological characteristics of judges as being essentially irrelevant to what is assumed to be significant in their official behavior. . . .

THE BEHAVIORAL APPROACH

Beginning about the middle of the 1950's, a third approach came to assume increasing importance in the study of judicial decision-making. The behavioral approach focuses upon the discrete human beings who act as judicial decision-makers. In particular, the behavioral approach investigates the socio-psychological dimensions of judicial decisions: How do the attitudes and belief systems of the judge as an individual affect his choices, and how do his personal relationships with other individuals affect his choices? Consequently, the family background, educational training and vocational experience, and political and religious affiliations of judges become relevant data for observation and analysis. Similarly, the social context of judicial choice must be explored: Who are the colleagues of an appellate court judge? How and to what extent is he influenced by them? How and why do the personal values of the judge enter into his official choices, emerging in the form of the "intent of the Constitutional fathers," of the legislature, or of a higher court?

Behavioralists assume that the study of "law" and "courts" should be undertaken as an aspect of modern social science. The cognate academic disciplines from which judicial behavior has borrowed most extensively, for theoretical and methodological guidance, have been psychology (for the analysis of individual judicial attitudes), sociology (for small-group analysis), and economics (for the analysis of rationality in decision-making). Behavioralists do not attempt to explain everything they observe in terms of a single concept, and they investigate questions that either would not or could not be studied systematically under either the traditional or the conventional approach. Perhaps the most important difference, however, is found in the insistence of the behavioralists upon employing explicit theoretical models, from which operationalized hypotheses can be inferred, to guide their empirical research. Statistical methods are used as the basis both for testing the significance of findings and for predicting future relationships on the basis of present knowledge about those that have obtained in the past. The ultimate test of the power of any science lies, of course, in its capacity to increase man's ability to anticipate future events and their probable consequences. In addition to explaining the past (as in the traditional approach) and describing the present (as in the conventional approach), the behavioral approach is concerned with predicting future developments in judicial behavior. . . .

SYSTEMS THEORY

This study of the judiciary is based upon an analytical framework known in sociology and political science as "systems theory" or "structural-functional analysis." This basis is chosen in preference to the legal, historical, and institutional categories that in the past have dominated inquiry into the policy-making processes of American government. A major advantage of this strategy is that it diverts attention both from a preoccupation with the substance of judicial policy and from a description of the legal structure of courts in isolation from the rest of the political system. Both of these subjects are relevant to an understanding of judicial policy-making; but the use of systems theory can, it is hoped, expand the relevant field of inquiry to the processes and sources of judicial policy-making as well as to its results. Thus this mode of analysis should facilitate a more general and more comprehensive examination of American judicial institutions and behavior than would be produced by a less inclusive and less consistent conceptual framework.

Systems analysis focuses upon political behavior and upon empirically observable action. Norms and institutions are relevant only to the extent that they affect the behavior of actors within a system under analysis. . . .

The model is "systemic" because it portrays certain functional interrelation-ships among stipulated structures; the relationships are ordered and are assumed to be relatively stable. The three structural components of the model are denoted as INPUT, CONVERSION, and OUTPUT units. . . .

The structures are linked by three sets of interaction processes. The INPUT and OUTPUT structures interact with the CONVERSION structure through *input* and *output* processes, respectively; the OUTPUT structure interacts with the IN-PUT structure through *feedback* processes. . . . [W]e can distinguish among the three theoretical approaches in the following way: traditional theory deals with univariate (OUTPUT) relationships, conventional theory with bivariate (IN-PUT–OUTPUT) relationships, and behavioral theory with multivariate (INPUT–CONVERSION–OUTPUT) relationships. . . .

POLICY INPUTS

We can readily distinguish several major classes of inputs for the Supreme Court. In the most direct and literal sense, demands emanate from litigants, although such demands usually are translated into the legal idiom before being presented to the Court by counsel who are specialists in translating lay interests (and empirical events) into legal language (and other forms of legal behavior). . . . A second general source of inputs is the record of the case itself and the briefs and oral argument presented to the Court. . . . Not only are there these authoritative suppositions about what happened before the trial began, but from the point of view of the Supreme Court, the events that transpired in the decision-making processes of the trial court and of the court of appeals also constitute a set of facts. . . . There is a third general source of inputs, the critics of the Court. Law schools provide the most important forum for professional criticism of all the national courts, including the Supreme Court. . . .

POLICY CONVERSION

According to our model . . . , the conversion structure is central in the judicial policy-making process. Conversion is the sub-process by means of which issues are recognized and decided as a result of group interaction and the integration of the values of the individual justices. The conversion structure consists of the values of the individual justices and the issues—their shared perceptions about the policy and factual questions raised by cases before them for a decision. In a formal sense, conversion as a process occurs when individual justices cast their votes on the disposition of a case at the group conference; and strictly speaking, the subsequent announcement both of the voting division of the Court, and of the opinions of the Court and of individual justices, are among the *outputs* of the conversion process. . . . [S]tudies of the

voting behavior of Supreme Court justices have shown that there are three
major attitudinal components of judicial
liberalism and conservatism. . . . The
three major attitudes are (1) *political*
liberalism and conservatism; (2) *economic* liberalism and conservatism; and
(3) *social* liberalism and conservatism.
. . . [P]olitical liberalism is the belief in
and the support of civil rights and liberties; political conservatism is the upholding of law and order and the defense of the status quo—no matter what
may be the pattern of accepted values
that the status quo happens to represent. Economic liberalism is the belief
in and the support of a more equal distribution of wealth, goods, and services;
the economic conservative defends private enterprise, vested interests, and
broad differentials in wealth and income between the owners of property
and laborers. A social liberal is a person who is liberal in both of the other
two attitudes and who therefore upholds
individual personal rights (political liberalism) but collective property rights
(economic liberalism); a social conservative upholds collective personal rights
but individual property rights. The social liberal favors change—disequilib-
rium—in regard to both personal and
property rights; the social conservative
favors the status quo—homeostasis—in

regard to both. It is easy to see, however, that it is quite possible for a judge
to feel that he is being consistent in his
ideology if he favors political liberalism
and economic conservatism, for this
combination of attitudes means to uphold both the personal and the property
rights of the individual. Similarly, a
justice who consistently upholds the
necessarily collectivized interests represented by the government will be politically conservative and economically liberal in his attitudes. . . .

One way to conceptualize the Supreme Court's output is in terms of the
policy norms that are associated with
the decisions in cases. . . . There are
three important sets of subcomponent
norms: political, social, and economic.
The political norms are the output coun-
terpart of the political liberalism attitudinal component; similarly, the economic norms are equivalent to positions
on the economic attitudinal variable.
The social norms correspond to an attitudinal position midway between political and economic liberalism. . . . Social
norms define the policy area in which
the Court's decisions have had the greatest impact upon the American polity
during the past two decades. Political
norms have been of secondary importance, while economic norms have been
relegated to last place. . . .

JUDICIAL ACTIVISM AND RESTRAINT

We are now in a position to suggest
a functional theory of judicial activism
and restraint. The Court's basic policies
remain stable over long periods of time,
and changes that do occur reflect very
fundamental changes in the general political system, of which the Court is a
component part. The justices themselves are goal oriented, and their basic
goals are the same as those that moti-
vate other political actors. Majority rule
among the justices determines the policy
goals that the Court supports, and it is
the underlying stability in the general
political system that accounts for the
continuity in the Court's policy-making,
by assuring that the judicial majority

will reflect the dominant majority in the
larger political system. If Supreme
Court justices were appointed for four-
year terms in phase with the presidential electoral cycle, then it could be
anticipated that there would be considerably less stability in the Court's policy-
making, because Court majorities would
be more responsive to the short-run
waves than to the long-run currents of
political change. Under our constitutional system, it is precisely at the times
of major realignment in the political
party system that the Supreme Court is
most likely to become involved in conspicuous and dramatic conflict with the
Presidency and the Congress, because

the majority of the justices then represent the minority in the new political realignment. . . .

[This] functional theory of judicial activism and restraint defines activism in terms of disharmony, and restraint in terms of harmony, between the policy of the Court and that of other decision-makers. We define "other decision-makers" quite broadly, to include (1) Congress, the President and administrative agencies, and lower national courts, and (2) the analogous officials of state governments. . . . According to this theory, the Court is activist whenever its policies are in *conflict* with those of other major decision-makers. . . . It should be clear both that this analysis applies irrespective of the substantive content of the policy at issue and that it applies equally to instances in which the Court's position is liberal and those in which it is conservative. . . . Judicial review, in the narrow sense of declarations by the Court that national or state legislation is unconstitutional, is simply one of the technical forms that judicial activism can assume when the Court finds itself in conflict with legislative policy-makers. When the Court majority takes one of the positions that we have classified as constituting restraint, it is possible, of course, for an individual justice or a minority of justices to behave as activists, in which event he or they will dissent from the decision of the majority. It follows that when a majority of the Court is activist, dissenters will argue in their opinions the virtues of judicial restraint, just as a majority will preach restraint to activist dissenters. Both of these types of behavior are readily observable in the opinions of the justices throughout the history of the

Court. As a relatively liberal justice, in regard to both civil liberties and economic issues, on an activist conservative Court, Holmes' frequently employed strategy of arguing judicial restraint (rather than the substantive merits of the issue) was quite rational and probably impaired the position of his more conservative colleagues much more effectively than a direct attack might have done. Holmes' famous dissent in *Lochner v. New York,* for example, did not quarrel (as Harlan did) with the majority on the question of whether a ten-hour day would be more healthful for employees in bakery sweat-shops than a sixteen-hour day; Holmes argued instead the proposition that, right or wrong, the state legislature rather than the United States Supreme Court had the constitutional right to establish policy on the question. On the other hand, a justice who utilizes the same argument in behalf of judicial restraint, at a time when the Court frequently is dominated by a majority of activist liberals, has no alternative but to dissent consistently in what functionally is a defense of conservative values. This is precisely the posture that was assumed during his last two decades as a Supreme Court justice by Frankfurter, an avowed proponent of both civil liberties and economic liberalism *before* he joined the Court but also an acknowledged student and avowed disciple of Holmes.

To summarize, from a functional point of view, the Court is activist when its decisions conflict with those of other political policy-makers, and the Court exercises restraint when it accepts the policies of other decision-makers. . . .

Do those decision makers always have the chance to decide

III. JUDICIAL RESTRAINT v. JUDICIAL ACTIVISM: TWO VIEWS ON THE ROLE OF THE JUDICIARY IN THE AMERICAN POLITICAL SYSTEM

The Case for Judicial Restraint

Learned Hand

WHEN A COURT SHOULD INTERVENE

Although Learned Hand was never on the Supreme Court, his judicial competence was universally recognized. While judge of the United States Circuit Court of Appeals for the 2nd Circuit, from 1924–1961, his opinions were regarded as authoritative, often by the Supreme Court itself.

I SHALL . . . ask you *arguendo* to assume with me that the Constitution and the "Bill of Rights" neither proceed from, nor have any warrant in, the Divine Will, either as St. Thomas or Jefferson believed; but on the contrary that they are the altogether human expression of the will of the state conventions that ratified them; that their authority depends upon the sanctions available to enforce them; and their meaning is to be gathered from the words they contain, read in the historical setting in which they were uttered. This presupposes that all political power emanates from the people, and that the Constitution distributed among different "Departments"—as Hamilton called them—the authority of each as it was measured by the grant to it. No provision was expressly made, however, as to how a "Department" was to proceed when in the exercise of one of its own powers it became necessary to consider the validity of some earlier act of another "Department." Should the second ac-

cept the decision of the first that the act was within the first's authority, or should it decide the question *de novo* according to its own judgment? A third view prevailed, as you all know: that it was a function of the courts to decide which "Department" was right, and that all were bound to accept the decision of the Supreme Court.

The arguments of those who, like Jefferson, held that each "Department" was free to decide the issues before it regardless of how any other "Department" had decided it, was, as I understand it, as follows: The exercise of any delegated power presupposes that the grantee believes that the grant extends to the occasion that has arisen; and it is a necessary incident of the grant itself that he shall so decide before he acts at all. He may of course be wrong; and, when he is, he will be accountable to the grantor; but he is accountable to no one else, unless it be an authority paramount to both himself and the grantor.

The federal courts themselves derive all their powers from the "People of the United States" when they "ordain[ed] and establish[ed]" the Constitution, and the same was true, *ceteris paribus*, of the state courts. One cannot find among the powers granted to courts any authority to pass upon the validity of the decisions of another "Department" as to the scope of that "Department's" powers. Indeed, it is to be understood that the three "Departments" were separate and coequal, each being, as it were, a Leibnizian monad, looking up to the Heaven of the Electorate, but without any mutual dependence. What could be better evidence of complete dependence than to subject the validity of the decision of one "Department" as to its authority on a given occasion to review and reversal by another whose own action was conditioned upon the answer to the same issue? Such a doctrine makes supreme the "Department" that has the last word. . . .

Before the other side definitively won its way in *Marbury v. Madison*, it had been equally vocal, in general as follows. In the first place, it was customary in colonial times for courts to decide whether colonial laws were in accord with colonial charters, and there were several instances after 1776 and before 1787 in which state courts had assumed the same authority as to state statutes. As the Constitution gradually took form in the Convention, again and again in their arguments, members assumed that the federal courts should have the same authority. One of the reasons against a "Council of Revision," of which the Supreme Court was to be a part, was that this would embarrass the exercise of its duty later to determine whether the Constitution had authorized the statute in question. It was the opinion at least of Gerry, Wilson, Mason, Morris, Hamilton, and, although the conclusion appears to me somewhat doubtful, perhaps also of Madison, that the Court was to decide whether a statute was within the powers of Congress. Finally, some decisions of the courts soon after 1789 are inconsistent with any other conclusion. In spite of authority which I am certainly not qualified to challenge, I cannot, however, help doubting whether the evidence justifies a certain conclusion that the Convention would have so voted, if the issue had been put to it that courts should have power to invalidate acts of Congress. It is significant that when Hamilton, who, as I have said, and as was in any event to be expected, had apparently been among those who supported the power, came to defend it as he did in the well-known 78th number of the Federalist, he did not suggest that the conclusion followed from anything in the text; but rather from the ordinary function of courts to construe statutes. The following is the meat of his argument:

It is far more rational to suppose that the courts were designed to be an intermediate body between the people and the legislature in order among other things to keep the latter within the limits assigned to their authority. The interpretation of the laws is the proper and peculiar province of the courts. A constitution is, in fact, and must be regarded by the judges, as a fundamental law. It therefore belongs to them to ascertain its meaning as well as the meaning of any particular act proceeding from the legislative body. . . . Nor does this conclusion by any means suppose a superiority of the judicial to the legislative power. It only supposes that the power of the people is superior to both; and that, where the will of the legislature declared in its statutes stands in opposition to that of the people declared by the Constitution, the judges ought to be governed by the latter rather than the former.

Obviously, Hamilton did not agree with Bishop Hoadley when in a sermon before George the First in 1717 he said: "Whoever hath an absolute authority to interpret written or spoken laws; it is he who is truly the lawgiver to all intents and purposes and not the person who wrote or spoke them."

It is interesting to observe how closely Marshall's reasoning in *Marbury v. Madison* followed Hamilton's.

It is, emphatically, the province and duty of the judicial department, to say what the law is. Those who apply the rule to particular cases, must of necessity expound and interpret that rule. If two laws conflict with each other, the courts must decide on the operation of each. So, if a law be in opposition to the constitution; if both the law and the constitution apply to a particular case, so that the court must either decide that case, conformable to the law, disregarding the constitution; or conformable to the constitution, disregarding the law; the court must determine which of these conflicting rules governs the case; this is of the very essence of judicial duty. If then, the courts are to regard the constitution, and the constitution is superior to any ordinary act of the legislature, the constitution, and not such ordinary act, must govern the case to which they both apply.

That reasoning had not always satisfied the Chief Justice, for in *Ware v. Hylton*, as counsel for the defendant he had expressed himself as follows:

The legislative authority of any country can only be restrained by its own municipal constitution; this is a principle that springs from the very nature of society; and the judicial authority can have no right to question the validity of a law, unless such a jurisdiction is expressly given by the constitution. It is not necessary to inquire, how the judicial authority should act, if the legislature were evidently to violate any of the laws of God; but property is the creature of civil society, and subject, in all respects, to the disposition and control of civil institutions. . . .

There was nothing in the United States Constitution that gave courts any authority to review the decisions of Congress; and it was a plausible—indeed to my mind an unanswerable—argument that it invaded that "Separation of Powers" which, as so many then believed, was the condition of all free government. That there were other reasons, not only proper but essential, for inferring such a power in the Constitution seems to me certain; but for the moment I am only concerned to show that the reasoning put forward to support the inference will not bear scrutiny.

As an approach, let us try to imagine what would have been the result if the power did not exist. There were two alternatives, each prohibitive, I submit. . . . [T]he first alternative would have meant that the interpretation of the Constitution on a given occasion would

be left to that "Department" before which the question happened first to come; and such a system would have been so capricious in operation, and so different from that designed, that it could not have endured. Moreover, the second alternative would have been even worse, for under it each "Department" would have been free to decide constitutional issues as it thought right, regardless of any earlier decision of the others. Thus it would have been the President's privilege, and indeed his duty, to execute only those statutes that seemed to him to be constitutional, regardless even of a decision of the Supreme Court. The courts would have entered such judgments as seemed to them consonant with the Constitution; but neither the President, nor Congress, would have been bound to enforce them if he or it disagreed, and without their help the judgments would have been waste paper.

For centuries it has been an accepted canon in interpretation of documents to interpolate into the text such provisions, though not expressed, as are essential to prevent the defeat of the venture at hand; and this applies with especial force to the interpretation of constitutions, which, since they are designed to cover a great multitude of necessarily unforeseen occasions, must be cast in general language, unless they are constantly amended. If so, it was altogether in keeping with established practice for the Supreme Court to assume an authority to keep the states, Congress, and the President within their prescribed powers. Otherwise the government could not proceed as planned; and indeed would almost certainly have foundered, as in fact it almost did over that very issue.

However, since this power is not a logical deduction from the structure of the Constitution but only a practical condition upon its successful operation, it need not be exercised whenever a court sees, or thinks that it sees, an invasion of the Constitution. It is always a preliminary question how importunately the occasion demands an answer. It may be better to leave the issue to be worked out without authoritative solution; or perhaps the only solution available is one that the court has no adequate means to enforce. . . .

The authority of courts to annul statutes (and *a fortiori*, acts of the Executive) may, and indeed must, be inferred, although it is nowhere expressed, for without it we should have to refer all disputes between the "Departments" and states to popular decision, patently an impractical means of relief, whatever Thomas Jefferson may have thought. However, this power should be confined to occasions when the statute or order was outside the grant of power to the grantee, and should not include a review of how the power has been exercised. This distinction in the case of legislation demands an analysis of its component factors. These are an estimate of the relevant existing facts and a forecast of the changes that the proposed measure will bring about. In addition it involves an appraisal of the values that the change will produce, as to which there are no postulates specific enough to serve as guides on concrete occasions. In the end all that can be asked on review by a court is that the appraisals and the choice shall be impartial. The statute may be far from the best solution of the conflicts with which it deals; but if it is the result of an honest effort to embody that compromise or adjustment that will secure the widest acceptance and most avoid resentment, it is "Due Process of Law" . . .

I have been only trying to say what is the measure of judicial intervention that can be thought to be implicit, though unexpressed, in the Constitution. You may well ask, however, what difference it makes at long last if the courts do exceed those implicit limits. Even though until about a century ago it was the accepted role of courts to confine themselves to occasions when Congress or the states had stepped over their borders, why should we now retreat, if it has become the custom to go further and correct patent deviations from a court's notions of justice? It is a "constitution," you may go on to remind me,

that we are "expounding," and constitutions have the habit of organic growth. Ours is no different from other constitutions, and it has by now been modified to protect the basic privileges of any free society by means of an agency made irresponsive to the pressure of public hysteria, public panic and public greed.

There may be much to be said for the existence of some such organ in a democratic state, especially if its power be confined to a suspensive veto, like that for example of the present British House of Lords. The recuperative powers of a government that has no such curb are indeed great, but in the interval between the damage and the restoration great permanent injury may be done, and in any event the suffering of individuals will never be repaired. Those who advocate such relief at times concede too scanty importance to the provisions very carefully devised at least in the federal Constitution to check hasty and ill-considered legislation. The veto and independent tenure of the President, unlike that of the ministry in most democracies, are obvious curbs upon sudden swings of popular obsession; so too is the Senate, whose control is in the hands of a small minority of the population, representing a facet of public opinion quite different from that of the urban sections. However, I am not going to discuss whether it might not be desirable to have a third chamber, but on the contrary I shall assume for argument that it would be. The question still remains whether the courts should be that chamber. . . .

We are faced with the ever-present problem in all popular government: how far the will of immediate majorities should prevail. Even assuming, as I am, that a suspensive veto would be desirable, the power to annul a statute is much more than that. It does not send back the challenged measure for renewed deliberation; it forbids it by making a different appraisal of the values, which, as I have just said, is the essence of legislation. Moreover, judges are seldom content merely to annul the particular solution before them; they do not, indeed they may not, say that taking all things into consideration, the legislators' solution is too strong for the judicial stomach. On the contrary they wrap up their veto in a protective veil of adjectives such as "arbitrary," "artificial," "normal," "reasonable," "inherent," "fundamental," or "essential," whose office usually, though quite innocently, is to disguise what they are doing and impute to it a derivation far more impressive than their personal preferences, which are all that in fact lie behind the decision. If we do need a third chamber it should appear for what it is, and not as the interpreter of inscrutable principles.

Another supposed advantage of the wider power of review seems to be that by "the moral radiation of its decision" a court may point the way to a resolution of the social conflicts involved better than any likely to emerge from a legislature. In other words, courts may light the way to a saner world and ought to be encouraged to do so. I should indeed be glad to believe it, and it may be that my failure hitherto to observe it is owing to some personal defect of vision; but at any rate judges have large areas left unoccupied by legislation within which to exercise this benign function. Besides, for a judge to serve as communal mentor appears to me a very dubious addition to his duties and one apt to interfere with their proper discharge. . . .

In the first place it is apparent, I submit, that insofar as it is made part of the duties of judges to take sides in political controversies, their known or expected convictions or predilections will, and indeed should, be at least one determinant in their appointment and an important one. There has been plenty of past experience that confirms this; indeed, we have become so used to it that we accept it as a matter of course. No doubt it is inevitable, however circumscribed his duty may be, that the personal proclivities of an interpreter will to some extent interject themselves into the meaning he imputes to a text, but in very much the greater part of a judge's duties he is charged with freeing himself as far as he can from all personal preferences, and that becomes difficult in proportion as these are strong. The degree to which he will secure compliance with his commands depends in large measure upon how far the community believes him to be the mouthpiece of a public will, conceived as the resultant of many conflicting strains that have come, at least provisionally, to a consensus. This sanction disappears insofar as it is supposed permissible for him covertly to smuggle into his decisions his personal notions of what is desirable, however disinterested personally those may be. Compliance will then much more depend upon a resort to force, not a desirable expedient when it can be avoided.

This consideration becomes especially important in appellate courts. It is often hard to secure unanimity about the borders of legislative power, but that is much easier than to decide how far a particular adjustment diverges from what the judges deem tolerable. On such issues experience has over and over again shown the difficulty of securing unanimity. This is disastrous because disunity cancels the impact of monolithic solidarity on which the authority of a bench of judges so largely depends. People become aware that the answer to the controversy is uncertain, even to those best qualified, and they feel free, unless especially docile, to ignore it if they are reasonably sure that they will not be caught. The reasoning of both sides is usually beyond their comprehension, and is apt to appear as verbiage designed to sustain one side of a dispute that in the end might be decided either way, which is generally the truth. Moreover, it certainly does not accord with the underlying presuppositions of popular government to vest in a chamber, unaccountable to anyone but itself, the power to suppress social experiments which it does not approve. Nothing, I submit, could warrant such a censorship except a code of paramount law that not only measured the scope of legislative authority but regulated how it should be exercised. . . . For myself it would be most irksome to be ruled by a bevy of Platonic Guardians, even if I knew how to choose them, which I assuredly do not. If they were in charge, I should miss the stimulus of living in a society where I have, at least theoretically, some part in the direction of public affairs. Of course I know how illusory would be the belief that my vote determined anything; but nevertheless when I go to the polls I have a satisfaction in the sense that we are all engaged in a common venture. If you retort that a sheep in the flock may feel something like it; I reply, following Saint Francis, "My brother, the Sheep.". . .

Wallace Mendelson

THE ORTHODOX, OR ANTI-ACTIVIST, VIEW
—MR. JUSTICE FRANKFURTER

A student of the thought of Justice Frankfurter, Wallace Mendelson, professor at the University of Texas, has defended his view of the role of the judiciary. Among his publications are *Discrimination* (1962), *Felix Frankfurter* (1964), and *Justices Black and Frankfurter: Confrontation in the Court* (1961).

JUDICIAL REVIEW has been a storm center in American history because it involves political choice without commensurate political responsibility. Oliver Wendell Holmes said:

. . . I think it most important to remember whenever a doubtful case arises with certain analogies on one side and other analogies on the other, that what really is before us is a conflict between two social desires, each of which seeks to extend its dominion over the case, and which cannot both have their way. . . . Where there is doubt the simple tool of logic does not suffice, and even if it is disguised and unconscious, the judges are called on to exercise the sovereign prerogative of choice.

The "great generalities" of the Due Process and the Commerce clauses, for example, can be judicially interpreted in the light of laissez-faire or the opposite. Either way, the people have no direct recourse, for federal judges are not answerable at the polls. As though recognizing this tension between judicial review and popular government, the Supreme Court has long since developed a series of self-restraining principles. Justice Louis Brandeis expressed their essence when he said, "The most important thing we do is not doing." What he meant, of course, is that the more the Court restrains itself, the greater are the freedom and responsibility of the people to govern themselves. He did not suggest that judicial review should be abandoned; after all, it is an established part of our constitutional system. But he recognized that standards for judgment are often vague; that the judiciary has very limited capacity to find and assess all of the data necessary for an informed judgment on the broad social issues behind the immediate claims of litigants; that judicial intervention in such matters is necessarily sporadic, indeed largely haphazard; that judges have no unique immunity from error; and that error in upholding a statute can be corrected by the people far more

Source: From *The Supreme Court: Law and Discretion*, edited by Wallace Mendelson. Copyright © 1967 by The Bobbs-Merrill Company, Inc., and reprinted by permission of the publishers.

readily than error raised to the status of a constitutional limitation. And so it is that Brandeis—like Justice Felix Frankfurter—was "forever disposing of issues by assigning [i.e., leaving] their disposition to some other [more politically responsible] sphere of competence." For ultra-activists this, of course, is nothing less than abdication of judicial duty.

Perhaps the most basic of the Court's self-restraining principles is avoidance of unnecessary constitutional commitments. After all, there is fatal "finality" in a decision on the meaning of the Constitution. The only legal way the people can change it is the cumbersome, minority-controlled process of formal amendment. And so, as Mr. Justice Brandeis summarized the ancient tradition:

Considerations of propriety, as well as long-established practice, demand that we refrain from passing upon the constitutionality of an act of Congress unless obliged to do so in the proper performance of our judicial function, when the question is raised by a party whose interests entitle him to raise it." *Blair v. United States,* 250 U.S. 273, 279. . . .

The Court has frequently called attention to the "great gravity and delicacy" of its function in passing upon the validity of an act of Congress; and has restricted exercise of this function by rigid insistence that the jurisdiction of federal courts is limited to actual cases and controversies; and that they have no power to give advisory opinions. On this ground it has in recent years ordered the dismissal of several suits challenging the constitutionality of important acts of Congress. . . .

The Court developed, for its own governance in the cases confessedly within its jurisdiction, a series of rules under which it has avoided passing upon a large part of all the constitutional questions pressed upon it for decision. They are:

1. The Court will not pass upon the constitutionality of legislation in a friendly, nonadversary, proceeding, declining because to decide such questions "is legitimate only in the last resort, and as a necessity in the determination of real, earnest, and vital controversy between individuals. It never was the thought that, by means of a friendly suit, a party beaten in the legislature could transfer to the courts an in-

quiry as to the constitutionality of the legislative act.". . .

2. The Court will not "anticipate a question of constitutional law in advance of the necessity of deciding it.". . . "It is not the habit of the court to decide questions of a constitutional nature unless absolutely necessary to a decision of the case.". . .

3. The Court will not "formulate a rule of constitutional law broader than is required by the precise facts to which it is to be applied.". . .

4. The Court will not pass upon a constitutional question although properly presented by the record, if there is also present some other ground upon which the case may be disposed of. This rule has found most varied application. Thus, if a case can be decided on either of two grounds, one involving a constitutional question, the other a question of statutory construction or general law, the Court will decide only the latter. . . . Appeals from the highest court of a state challenging its decision of a question under the federal Constitution are frequently dismissed because the judgment can be sustained on an independent state ground. . . .

5. The Court will not pass upon the validity of a statute upon complaint of one who fails to show that he is injured by its operation. . . . Among the many applications of this rule, none is more striking than the denial of the right of challenge to one who lacks a personal or property right. Thus, the challenge by a public official interested only in the performance of his official duty will not be entertained. . . . In *Fairchild v. Hughes,* 258 U.S. 126, the Court affirmed the dismissal of a suit brought by a citizen who sought to have the Nineteenth Amendment declared unconstitutional. In *Massachusetts v. Mellon,* 262 U.S. 447, the challenge of the federal Maternity Act was not entertained although made by the commonwealth on behalf of all its citizens.

6. The Court will not pass upon the constitutionality of a statute at the instance of one who has availed himself of its benefits. . . .

7. "When the validity of an act of Congress is drawn in question, and even if a serious doubt of constitutionality is raised, it is a cardinal principle that this Court will first ascertain whether a construction of the statute is fairly possible by which the question may be avoided.". . .

A related principle finds expression in the doctrine of political questions. It holds that courts should avoid involvement in matters traditionally left to legislative policy-making; in matters as to which there are no adequate constitutional standards to guide judicial judgment; or in matters as to which there are no adequate modes of judicial relief. In *Coleman v. Miller,* for example, the Court was asked to decide whether a proposed constitutional amendment had expired simply because it had not been ratified by three-fourths of the states in a "reasonable" period of time. Refusing decision, the Court said:

. . . Where are to be found the criteria for such a judicial determination? None are to be found in the Constitution or statute. . . . When a proposed amendment springs from a conception of economic needs, it would be necessary, in determining whether a reasonable time had elapsed since its submission, to consider [among other things] the economic conditions prevailing in the country, whether these had so far changed since the submission as to make the proposal no longer responsive to the conception which inspired it or whether conditions were such as to intensify the feeling of need and the appropriateness of the proposed remedial action. In short, the question of a reasonable time . . . would involve . . . appraisal of a great variety of relevant conditions, political, social, and economic which can hardly be said to be within the appropriate range of evidence receivable in a court of justice. . . . On the other hand, these conditions are appropriate for the consideration of the political departments of the government.

Another principle of judicial restraint recognizes, as Chief Justice John Marshall said, that "The question, whether a law be void for repugnancy to the Constitution, is, at all times, a question of much delicacy, which ought seldom, if ever, to be decided in the affirmative in a doubtful case." As Mr. Justice Washington put it a few years later:

. . . the [constitutional] question which I have been examining is involved in difficulty and doubt. But if I could rest my opinion in favor of the constitutionality of the law . . . on no other ground than this doubt . . . that alone would . . . be a satisfactory vindication of it. It is but a decent respect due to the wisdom, the integrity,

and the patriotism of the legislative body, by which any law is passed, to presume in favor of its validity, until its violation of the Constitution is proved beyond all reasonable doubt. This has always been the language of this Court . . . and I know it expresses the honest sentiments of each and every member of the bench.

In this view, a legislative act may be held invalid only when the Court is prepared to say that no reasonable mind could uphold the legislative view. For doubt entails choice, and in a democracy choice is the province of the people. This rule of doubt is related to the common-law guide—the reasonable man. Who is this creature? Like jury and legislature, he symbolizes all of us. He is an "external standard," an American Everyman, whereby the troubled judge seeks to guard against his own personal bias in favor of the "views and feelings that may fairly be deemed representative of the community as a continuing society."

Behind all these self-denying ordinances of the orthodox tradition lies a common principle: Government by the judiciary is a poor substitute for government by the people. With this and its supporting doctrines there has been all but universal agreement, on and off the bench. Thus it may be fairly called the orthodox view, though in practice it is not equally respected by all judges. The anti-activist is perhaps a bit more concerned, and a bit more successful, than others in distinguishing between "law" and his own heart's desire. In this no one can hope to be completely successful, yet we know as a matter of experience that some men—on or off the bench—achieve much more objectivity than others. Mr. Justice Frankfurter's opinion in the second *Flag Salute* case is no doubt the classic modern expression of the anti-activist approach.

When Professor Frankfurter left Harvard for the bench in 1939, he was generally considered a liberal—in some quarters even a radical. More recently, he has been accused of conservatism. Yet it seems clear that his basic outlook did not change. In private life he was one of the great liberals of our day. But it is crucial in his philosophy that a judge's private convictions are one thing, his duty on the bench quite another. This was the teaching of Holmes. By failing to heed it, the proprietarians among the "nine old men" destroyed the old Court—just as the libertarians might have destroyed the new one, if they had had enough votes to do so. As both professor and judge, with respect to both liberty and property, Felix Frankfurter was skeptical of government by the judiciary. The judge's job, as he understood it, is to decide "cases" and "controversies," not to create a brave new world—for the legislative function has been given to others:

. . . As society becomes more and more complicated and individual experience correspondingly narrower, tolerance and humility in passing judgment on the experience and beliefs expressed by those entrusted with the duty of legislating emerge as the decisive factors in . . . adjudication.

He found strange indeed the neo-activist conception of democracy which holds that the people may be trusted with relatively unimportant things but not with those deemed crucial; i.e., with economic problems but not with those of civil liberty.

It is not that the Justice loved liberty less, but rather that he loved democracy —*in all its aspects*—more. The difficulty is that both individual freedom and majority rule are indispensable in the democratic dream. Yet neither can fully prevail without destroying the other. To reconcile them is the basic problem of free government. Chief Justice Stone put it briefly:

. . . There must be reasonable accommodation between the competing demands of freedom of speech and religion on the one hand, and other interests of society which have some claims upon legislative protection. To maintain the balance between them is essential to the well-ordered functioning of government under a constitution. Neither is absolute, and neither can constitutionally be made the implement for the destruction of the other. That is where the judicial function comes in.

Mr. Justice Frankfurter could not believe or pretend that reconciliation is achieved via word-play with cliché like "liberty of contract" or "freedom of speech." The single-value, conditioned reflex gave him no respite from the painful process of judgment. For he knew, with Holmes, that his own "certitude was not the test of certainty"—that when legislatures disagreed with him they might be right. It followed that judicial intrusion upon the extrajudicial processes of government was permissible only in accordance with that ancient tradition of restraint which all American judges have professed—when their particular "preferred place" values were not at stake.

Obviously Mr. Justice Frankfurter found the crux of the democratic process not so much in its immediate legislative product as in the educative and tension-relieving role of the process itself. A generation ago he wrote:

. . . In a democracy, politics is a process of popular education—the task of adjusting the conflicting interests of diverse groups, . . . and bending the hostility and suspicion and ignorance engendered by group interests . . . toward mutual understanding.

To frustrate these pragmatic political accommodations by judicial absolutes is to frustrate our chief device for maintaining peace among men who are deeply divided—sometimes even in their conceptions of right and wrong. Moreover, "holding democracy in judicial tutelage is not the most promising way to foster disciplined responsibility in a free people."

It is ironical that Mr. Justice Frankfurter is now condemned by some for the very quality that won him a seat on the bench—respect for the political processes. It is even more ironical that, for essentially the same approach that earned the conservative Holmes a liberal reputation, the liberal Frankfurter is now deemed by some a conservative. What has changed, of course, is the relative liberalism of Court and legislatures. But in Felix Frankfurter's view the people's representatives are due equal deference, be they liberal or conservative. He saw as an abiding democratic principle what some find merely a gambit in the great game of power politics.

One need not insist that the Justice never fell short of his own goal. But surely his defections were few, and it may be that he left more choices to the people than has any other great modern judge (except, perhaps, Learned Hand). If this is abdication—as some insist when their "preferred place" values are at stake—it is abdication in favor of "the exhilarating adventure of a free people determining its own destiny."

Plainly Felix Frankfurter was always uneasy with judicial supremacy—whether with respect to personal interests called property, or those called liberty. Of course, the people may go wrong (whatever that means ultimately). Yet, in his view, "to fail and learn by failure is one of the sacred rights of a democracy."

Here, no doubt, is the heart of the matter. Behind all the subtle complexity of his jurisprudence lay a patient confidence in the people. He completely rejected what Professor Berman calls the "underlying assumptions" of Soviet law —that "the citizen is not a mature, independent adult . . . but an immature, dependent child or youth. . . ." And so, from first to last, Felix Frankfurter was wary of judicial efforts to impose Justice on the people—to force upon them "better" government than they were able at the moment to give themselves. It was his deepest conviction that no five men, or nine, are wise enough or good enough to wield such power over an entire nation. Morris R. Cohen put it bluntly: If judges are to govern, they ought to be elected.

The Case for Judicial Activism

Alpheus Thomas Mason

THE WARREN COURT AND THE BILL OF RIGHTS

A prolific scholar on the Court, Alpheus Thomas Mason, McCormick professor of jurisprudence at Princeton, has written Harlan Fiske Stone: Pillar of the Law (1956), The Brandeis Way (1933), Brandeis—Lawyer and Judge in the Modern State (1933), Brandeis: A Free Man's Life (1945), The Supreme Court: Instrument of Power or of Revealed Truth? (1953), The States' Rights Debate (1964), Free Government in the Making (1965), The Supreme Court from Taft to Warren (1959), William Howard Taft: Chief Justice (1965), and The Supreme Court: Palladium of Freedom (1962). Also, with W. B. Beaney, he wrote, The Supreme Court in a Free Society (1959), and edited, American Constitutional Law, fourth edition (1968). With R. H. Leach, he wrote, In Quest of Freedom: American Political Thought and Practice (1959).

THE WARREN COURT, now in its fourteenth year, belies Hamilton's relaxed portrayal of the Supreme Court as a weakling and Chief Justice Marshall's incredible description of the judicial function as involving only judgment, not will. Jefferson and Madison had envisaged a more positive role for the Judiciary. They had anticipated with warm approval that it would act

Source: The Yale Review, Vol. LVI, No. 2 (Winter 1967), pp. 197–211. Copyright Yale University.

creatively in the enforcement of the Bill of Rights. Yet Chief Justice Warren's unshakable conviction that the Bill of Rights is "the heart of any constitution" evokes fierce attack even from his colleagues.

Two basic issues divide the Warren Court: first, the relative claims of the Bill of Rights on the one hand, and federalism and separation of powers on the other, to judicial guardianship as bulwarks of freedom; second, whether economic dogma, such as laissez-faire, has any greater claim to judicial consideration than political ideology—"one man, one vote," "unrestrained egalitarianism." In 1873, and for many years thereafter, Justice Field, disregarding the claims of federalism, took up the cudgels in favor of economic dogma as a spur for economic enterprise. Pitted against Field was Justice John M. Harlan, grandfather of the present Justice Harlan, who affirmed Congressional guardianship of civil liberties. In the civil rights cases of 1883, he foreshadowed the school desegregation decisions of the 1950's and the constitutionality of the 1964 Civil Rights Act. In his *Hurtado* dissent of 1884, he anticipated Justice Black's increasingly successful campaign to bring the entire Bill of Rights under the broad umbrella of the Fourteenth Amendment. Nor was Justice Harlan content merely to rely on the naked provisions of the Constitution. He cited a justifying "penumbra" of political theory—"the great and essential principles of free government."

At the present moment the Bill of Rights and the elder Harlan's heightened concept of judicial duty are in the ascendancy (but one notes that his dissenting grandson has recently won support from activist Justice Black).

The present Justice Harlan's dissents revive the eighteenth-century debate between Federalists and anti-Federalists as to whether a bill of rights was a necessary supplement to the protection afforded by federalism and separation of powers. Also rejuvenated is a variant of "dual federalism," the doctrine that certain subject matter, notably the administration of criminal justice, is peculiarly within the domain of the states. Justice Harlan's position also recalls the charges dissenters Holmes and Stone hurled against the Court when, in deference to economic theory, the Justices vetoed government regulation of the economy. In 1905, Holmes protested that the Constitution must not be equated with any particular *economic* theory; in 1966 Justice Harlan insists that the Constitution embodies no particular *political* theory. "One man, one vote" is, he declares, a judicial creation, a "political theory," "a piece of political ideology," reflecting "the Court's view of what is constitutionally permissible."

For Justice Harlan the ruling that seats in both houses of a bicameral state legislature must be apportioned on a population basis is "an experiment in venturesome constitutionalism," "a radical alteration in the relationship between the states and the Federal Government," the substitution of the Court's view "of what should be so for the amending process." "The Constitution is not," he insists, "a panacea for every blot on the public welfare, nor should this Court, ordained as a judicial body, be thought of as a general haven for reform movements." Harlan upbraids the majority generally for assuming that "deficiencies in society which have failed of correction by other means should find a cure in courts." His continuing complaint is that the Warren Court, enamored of the Bill of Rights and egalitarianism, "has forgotten the sense of judicial restraint which, with due regard for *stare decisis*, is one element that should enter into deciding whether a past decision of this Court should be overruled."

Nor does this charge of judicial usurpation stem solely from so-called neutralists. At the Court's session of June 7, 1965, Justice Black, parting company with his erstwhile activist colleague, William O. Douglas, objected to judicial creation of a power-blocking "penumbra," reading the "right to privacy" into several provisions of the Bill of Rights. General application of the constitutional right of privacy would, he said, "amount to a great unconstitutional shift of power to the Courts," tending to break down separation of powers and federalism.

The critical reactions of the Justices recall earlier complaints. No Court has escaped Jefferson's charge of working "like gravity" to enlarge its jurisdiction. This note—abuse of power, the peril of judges stepping into the shoes of legislators—has been sounded throughout our history. Judicial history is repeating itself but, although the Warren Court's dramatic intervention in the governing process echoes 1920–1936 in boldness, there is no parallel in the ends served. More illuminating antecedents may be found in the constitutional jurisprudence of John Marshall. Like the bench Chief Justice Marshall headed (1803–1835), the Warren Court is stirring powerful currents in our politics. Just as Marshall's fervent nationalism stirred violent criticism in the Democratic Republican (as opposed to the Federalist) party, so the Warren Court's defense of basic freedoms rouses bitter denunciation from those inclined to equate security with repression.

Chief Justice Marshall, at the end of his long judicial career, boasted that his Court had "never sought to enlarge judicial power beyond its proper bounds nor feared to carry it to the fullest extent duty requires." Sensitive to the narrow line that separates judicial *review* and judicial *supremacy*, Marshall thought he had met the demanding requirements of both *self-restraint* and judicial *duty.* The provisions of the Constitution must neither be "restricted into insignificance, nor extended to objects not comprehended in them nor contemplated by its framers."

Judicial review, like the Constitution itself, affirms as well as negates; it is both a power-releasing and power-braking function. "The restraining power of the judiciary," Judge Cardozo wrote in 1921, "does not manifest its chief worth in the few cases in which the legislature has gone beyond the lines that mark the limits of discretion. Rather shall we find its chief worth in making vocal and audible the ideals that might otherwise be silenced, in giving them continuity of life and of expression in guiding and directing choice within the limits where choice ranges." John Marshall deserves to be remembered as much, if not more, for *McCulloch v. Maryland,* in which the Court affirmed the power of Congress to incorporate a bank, nontaxable by the State, thus laying the foundations of national power, as for *Marbury v. Madison,* in which, for the first time, the Court set aside an act of Congress.

Chief Justice Marshall insisted that judicial duty is heightened when political checks are ineffective or unavailable. When a state, as in *McCulloch v. Maryland,* taxes an instrumentality of the national government, "it acts upon institutions created, not by their own constituents, but by people over whom they claim no control." Since the people of the United States were not represented in the Maryland legislature which enacted the offending law, the usual political restraints for correcting abuse of power were not operative, hence an enlarged judicial responsibility. Holding that the Supreme Court's primary task is positive and creative, Chief Justice Marshall deplored any construction which attempts "to explain away the Constitution," leaving it "a magnificent structure . . . to look at, but totally unfit for use." The Judiciary, like other agencies of government, should facilitate achievement of the great objectives mentioned in the Constitution's Preamble.

Professor James Bradley Thayer, noting that Constitutional law "is allied, not merely with history, but with statecraft," singled out Chief Justice Marshall as one among a handful of American judges who were "sensible of the true nature of their work and of the large method of treatment which it required, who perceived that our constitutions had made them, in a limited and secondary way, but a real one, coadjutors with the other departments in the business of government; but many have fallen short of the requirements of so great a function." History may list Earl Warren among the few who met the test.

Judicial review as a barrier against governing reached a high point in the middle 1930's. Of the eighty-eight Congressional Statutes declared unconstitutional throughout our history, eleven fell under the judicial axe in 1935–1936. The resulting impasse between Court and legislature provoked President Roosevelt's disingenuous war on the Judiciary. The upshot was sudden judicial about-face, with massive breakdown of constitutional limitations—separation of powers, federalism, "due process of law," judicial review itself—previously invoked against government regulation of the economy. Soon thereafter a new direction emerged stressing judicial duty and responsibility. The judicial activism of the Hughes Court—to prevent social and economic experimentation—is now recognized as indefensible and self-defeating. Under Chief Justice Warren, as during John Marshall's long regime, the Supreme Court has become again a creative force in American life.

The late Professor Corwin of Princeton called the ignominious judicial somersault of 1937 "Constitutional Revolution, Limited." He predicted that the Justices would pay thereafter greater deference to the policy-forming organs of government and be less concerned with the wisdom of social and economic legislation. Corwin suggested that the Court, having abandoned guardianship of property, would still have plenty to do if it intervened "on behalf of the helpless and oppressed"; it would then "be free, as it has not in many years, to support the humane values of free thought, free utterance, and fair play." Surrender of its role as protector of economic privilege would allow the Court "to give voice to the conscience of the country." These prophetic words, reminiscent of Jefferson's argument of 1789 in favor of a bill of rights—the "legal check" it places in the hands of the Judiciary—were written in 1940. Looking back as well as ahead, Corwin noted in 1941: "Constitutional law has always a central interest to guard."

The Warren Court has provoked widespread criticism. At issue among the Justices are basic constitutional verities —federalism and the Bill of Rights—

and the Court's responsibility toward them. Upholding values long identified with the late Justice Frankfurter, Justice Harlan deplores what he considers the majority's mad rush to bring an ever-increasing number of Bill of Rights provisions under the equal protection and due process clauses of the Fourteenth Amendment—at the expense of federalism and separation of powers— values which, he insists, "lie at the root of our constitutional system."

"We are accustomed," Justice Harlan says, "to speak of the Bill of Rights and the Fourteenth Amendment as the principal guarantees of personal liberty. Yet it would surely be shallow not to recognize that the structure of our political system accounts no less for the free society we have." The founding fathers "staked their faith that liberty would prosper in the new nation not primarily upon declarations of individual rights but upon the kind of government the Union was to have." "No view of the Bill of Rights or interpretation of any of its provisions," he warns, "which fails to take due account of [federalism and separation of powers] can be considered constitutionally sound."

For Justice Harlan, the decisions asserting judicial responsibility for "one man, one vote" "cut deeply into the fabric of our federalism," representing entry into an area "profoundly ill-advised and constitutionally impermissible." Echoing the concern voiced in 1873, when the Court refused to become, under the sweeping provisions of the Fourteenth Amendment, "a perpetual censor upon all legislation of the states," Harlan believes that the end achieved would be "at the cost of a radical alteration in the relationship between the states and the federal government, more particularly the federal judiciary." Extending to accused persons in state courts the safeguards available to them in the federal courts is denounced as "historically and constitutionally unsound and incompatible with the maintenance of our federal system."

"It is the very essence of American federalism," Justice Harlan wrote in

1958, "that the States should have the widest latitude in the administration of their own system of criminal justice." He insists that such diversity is inherent in federalism. Judicial censorship of obscene and indecent literature entrenches on the "prerogative of the states to differ on their ideas of morality," denying both nation and states the advantage of having fifty laboratories of experimentation for trying out "different attitudes toward the same work of literature."

On April 5, 1965, shortly before he doffed judicial robes to become Ambassador to the United Nations, Justice Goldberg made a point-by-point reply to Justice Harlan. Goldberg noted that Harlan's bugaboo, his grandfather's and Justice Black's "incorporation" theory, had made notable progress. Now included among the Fourteenth Amendment's guarantees against infringement by the states are the liberties of the First, Fourth, Fifth, Sixth, and Eighth amendments. Goldberg did not accept Justice Harlan's easy transition from Brandeis' claims for the advantages of federalism in the field of economics to the area of civil rights. "While I agree with Justice Brandeis," Goldberg observed tartly, "that it is one of the happy incidents of the federal system that . . . a state may . . . serve as a laboratory, and try novel social and economic experiments . . . I do not believe that this includes the power to experiment with the fundamental liberties of citizens safeguarded by the Bill of Rights."

Nor did Justice Goldberg believe that Harlan's restrictive view of judicial duty would advance any legitimate state interest. Said Goldberg: "to deny to the states the power to impair a fundamental constitutional right is not to increase federal power, but, rather, to limit the power of both federal and state governments in favor of safeguarding the fundamental rights and liberties of the individual." Since *Gideon v. Wainwright,* guaranteeing a Florida indigent his constitutional right to counsel, twenty-six states have instituted vital reforms in their criminal procedure. "I didn't start

out," the triumphant Clarence Gideon observes, "to do anything for anybody but myself, but this decision has done a helluva lot of good."

The day when law enforcement officers could do pretty much as they pleased is now past. *Mapp* (1961) holds that evidence obtained by search and seizure in violation of the Fourth Amendment is inadmissible in a state court, as in a federal court; *Escobedo* (1964) guarantees the right to counsel under the Sixth and Fourteenth Amendments; *Miranda et al.* (1966) extends the privilege against self-incrimination to the police station. Justice Harlan dissented in all these cases. Pleading the necessity of preserving "a proper balance between state and federal responsibility in the administration of criminal justice," he denounces the new rules as a "hazardous experimentation." "The Court," Harlan warns, "is taking a real risk with society's welfare in imposing its new regime on the country." He believes the new rules are "ill-conceived and seriously and unjustifiably fetter perfectly legitimate methods of criminal law enforcement."

Goldberg was unconvinced. In answer to complaints that police chiefs and district attorneys are being handcuffed in the performance of their duties, he retorted:

No system worth preserving should have to *fear* that if an accused is permitted to consult with a lawyer, he will become aware of, and exercise these rights. If the exercise of constitutional rights will thwart the effectiveness of a system of law enforcement, then there is something very wrong with that system.

Nor has more equitable representation, in response to judicial command, weakened the states, or encouraged, as Justice Harlan anticipated, "inertia in efforts for political reform through the political process." In May, 1966, the Council of State Government reported that thirty-seven states, under court orders, had reapportioned one or more houses of their legislatures. In time, reapportionment, advancing on a broad front, may better equip the states to meet twentieth-century needs, revitalizing rather than disabling these essential units of local government.

In June, 1965, Justice Harlan's campaign for judicial self-restraint won significant though qualified support from Justice Black, previously a fierce antagonist. Speaking for the Court in *Griswold v. Connecticut*, Justice Douglas invoked amendments One, Three, Four, Five, Six, Nine, and Fourteen. In none, however, was there a specific bar against Connecticut's anticontraceptive statute. Douglas found the constitutional killer in the right of privacy, in "penumbras formed by emanations from those guarantees that give them life and substance." The right of privacy, the majority's spokesman declared, is "older than our political parties, older than our school system." This was too much for Justice Black. In dissent, he recalled the danger of falling into the judicial trap from which the Court had narrowly extricated itself in 1937—the ever-seductive snare of judicial preeminence. "Subjective consideration of 'natural' justice," Black warned, "is no less dangerous when used to enforce this Court's views about personal rights than those about economic rights." Black cautioned against reinstating *Lochner* "and other cases from which this Court recoiled in 1937." Apparently, the dissenting Justice noted, "my Brethren have less quarrel with economic regulations than former Justices of their persuasion had." For Justice Black, "penumbra" of whatever orientation permits judges to enforce their predilections as law.

Justices Black and Harlan dissented again in the 6 to 3 decision, March 24, 1966, declaring unconstitutional the Virginia poll tax as a voting qualification. In protest against reading current political theory into the Constitution, Justice Harlan wrote:

Property and poll-tax qualifications, very simply, are not in accord with current egalitarian notions of how a modern democracy should be organized. It is of course entirely fitting that legislatures should modify the law to reflect such changes in popular attitudes. However, it is all wrong, in my view, for the Court to adopt the political doctrines popularly accepted at a particular moment of our history and to declare all others to be irrational and invidious, barring them from the range of choice by reasonably minded people acting through the political process. It was not too long ago that Mr. Justice Holmes felt impelled to remind the Court that the Due Process Clause of the Fourteenth Amendment does not enact the laissez-faire theory of society. . . . The times have changed, and perhaps it is appropriate to observe that neither does the Equal Protection Clause of that Amendment rigidly impose upon America an ideology of unrestrained egalitarianism.

Like Harlan, Justice Black objected to the Court's use of the Equal Protection Clause "to write into the Constitution its notions of what it thinks is good governmental policy." The majority had found adherence to the original meaning of the Constitution "an intolerable and debilitating evil." It believed "that our Constitution should not be 'shackled to the political theory of a particular era,' and that to save the country from the original Constitution the Court must have constant power to renew it and keep it abreast with this Court's more enlightened theories of what is best for our society." Black declared war on this approach:

When a "political theory" embodied in our Constitution becomes outdated . . . a majority of the nine members of this Court are not only without constitutional power but are far less qualified to choose a new constitutional political theory than the people of this country proceeding in the manner provided by Article V.

Justice Black's dissenting opinion in the poll-tax case continues the campaign he launched in 1947 against the "natural justice formula" which he had himself once endorsed (and of which Justice Harlan approves), permitting Supreme Court Justices to pick and choose what provisions of the Bill of Rights are incorporated into the Fourteenth Amendment. Under this formula, the Court is licensed, Black declares, "to roam at large in the broad expanses of policy and morals and to trespass, all too freely, on the legislative domain of the states as well as the federal government." Black would narrow the range of judicial discretion by extending "to all the people of the nation the complete protection of the Bill of Rights." Justice Black, resting apparently under the comfortable illusion that the provisions of the Bill of Rights are mathematically precise, seems to believe that their incorporation into the Fourteenth Amendment would leave no room for theorizing or judicial choice.

The role of the Judiciary in a free society and the dichotomy concerning judicial restraint and judicial duty are at issue within the Court and in the country. The late Justice Frankfurter held that "judicial review is itself a limitation on popular government." Of course it is, and that is precisely what the framers intended it to be. But any implication that judicial review is therefore suspect as an alien intruder is mistaken. An informed student of the American political tradition might rewrite Frankfurter's statement: "Judicial review is but one among several auxiliary precautions the framers considered essential to the functioning of the American system of free government"; or, in the late Edward S. Corwin's epigram, judicial review is "democracy's way of covering its bet." "Those who won our independence," Justice Brandeis noted in 1927, "recognizing the occasional tyrannies of governing majorities . . . amended the Constitution so that free speech and assembly should be guaranteed."

The shift from constitutional limitations, featuring federalism and separation of powers, applied prior to 1937 to economic regulations, and to constitutional limitations and affirmations grounded in the Bill of Rights, is reflected in a host of Warren Court rulings. In the 1935–1936 term, there were 160 decisions in which opinions were written. Of these, only two were in the area of civil rights and liberties. Cases dealing with civil liberties now claim the lion's share of the Court's work load. In 1960–1961, 54 of the 120

decisions in which opinions were prepared concerned civil rights and liberties. There were 28 such cases in 1961–1962, 42 in 1962–1963, 45 in 1965–1966. These figures afford a measure of the Warren Court's dynamic role in giving reality to the Bill of Rights. Fulfilled is Jefferson's and Madison's forecast of 1789, that enforcement of the Bill of Rights would become the special concern of the Judiciary.

The record of the Constitution's framing and ratification clearly reveals an intention to establish *free government*. It was recognized, as Hamilton said in *Federalist* No. 22, that "the fabric of American empire ought to rest on the solid basis of the Consent of the People." But a complexus of principles and devices—federalism, separation of powers, bills of rights, judicial review—restrain popular power and limit majority rule. The electorate, through its chosen representatives, can make government conform to its will. But the Constitution sets bounds, enforceable by nine politically nonresponsible men. The resulting dilemma was once resolved by recourse to the patent fiction that the Court has no power; it merely applies the Constitution which, in some miraculous way, is always the highest expression of the people's will. This ancient theory no longer satisfies. In the middle 1930's, when nine men, sometimes only five or six, defeated the power to govern at all levels, very nearly the last vestige of judicial mysticism vanished. Before the astonished eyes of critics and friends, the judicial veil was lifted. Government was allowed to govern.

Control of our economic life, unprecedented in scope, made the equitable and unimpeded functioning of the political process more important than ever before. The right to vote, "a fundamental political right, because it is preservative of all rights," is only the last step in a long development. Informed political action would be impossible if the climate of opinion discouraged free exchange of ideas. Without equal opportunity to utilize the crucial preliminaries —speech, press, assembly, petition— government by consent becomes an empty declamation. In a free society, majorities are always in flux. Tomorrow's majority may have a different composition and therefore different goals. Defense of the political rights of minorities thus becomes, not the antithesis of majority rule, but its very foundation. The majority must leave open the political channels by which it can be replaced when no longer able to command popular support. The alternative is violent overthrow—revolution. By protecting the integrity and unobstructed operation of the process by which majorities are formed, judicial review becomes a surrogate for revolution, contributing positively to government resting on consent.

The contradiction Judge Learned Hand thought he detected in the position of the new activists—tolerance toward experimental legislation in economics, closer judicial scrutiny when First Amendment and other Bill of Rights freedoms are involved—is not that at all. More exacting supervision of the political process follows logically from the Court's greater reliance, after 1937, on political controls in the economic realm. This rationale derives strength not only from the Constitution's framers but also from a host of judicial luminaries in our own time, including Holmes, Brandeis, Hughes, Cardozo, and Stone.

It is often said that the Supreme Court reflects the social conscience of a nation. In the desegregation decisions and others, including the rulings on reapportionment and right to counsel, the Warren Court has not only interpreted and enforced the social conscience, it has quickened it. In the abstract, it would have been better, perhaps, if encroachment on individual freedom, such as Connecticut's anticontraceptive statute, Virginia's poll tax, and the police-state methods used in law enforcement, could have been remedied by state legislation. But this was not done; the prospects were dim. As in school desegregation, reapportionment, and administration of criminal justice, failure of the states to protect individual liberties, or undertake corrective measures,

drove the Court, in the face of delimiting precedents, into untrod fields. The Justices faced an untoward condition, not a theory. Judge Cardozo, noting that *stare decisis* is not in the Constitution, expressed "willingness to put it there . . . if only it were true that legislation is a sufficient agency of growth."

American constitutionalism's theme remains unchanged—that the individual and his freedom are basic. But the content of these values is altered. Formerly the Court assumed special guardianship of property and contract rights. These were *the* preferred freedoms. Now the Judiciary seems content to leave these to the mercy of political controls. Another category of preferred freedoms is accorded more exacting scrutiny today—speech, press, and religion, the right to vote, the rights of the criminally accused, the rights of discrete and insular racial, religious, and national minorities helpless in the face of a majority (or a minority) bent on curbing their freedom. Just as the Court formerly claimed preeminence as protector of tangible rights, so today it asserts special responsibility toward moral and spiritual values that lie at the base of our culture. Judicial concern for human values is recent. Reflecting on the constitutional jurisprudence of the 1920's, Professor Frankfurter said:

That a majority of the Court which frequently disallowed restraints on economic power should so consistently have sanctioned restraints of the mind is perhaps only a surface paradox. There is an underlying unity between fear of ample experimentation in economics and fear of expression of heretical ideas.

Not least among the distinctive accomplishments of the Warren Court is its alertness to a subtlety to which Justice Frankfurter, ignoring the commanding lessons of his mentors Holmes and Brandeis, seemed insensitive. In the face of vigorous protest from Justices Frankfurter and Harlan, our fourteenth Chief Justice has, in Judge Cardozo's words, made "vocal and audible ideals that might otherwise be silenced." Thanks to judicial review, "revolution" has been domesticated, brought within the four corners of the Constitution. Oppression of individuals and minorities may encourage resort to the moral right of revolution, a right no American can gracefully query; an independent Judiciary, by courageously interposing its judgment against majorities bent on infractions of the Constitution, advances the cause of peaceful change. In America "vibrations of power" (the "genius" of our system for Hamilton) are institutionalized; the pendulum may swing freely, reflecting alternating moods and responses about man and society. With peaceful remedies available for the correction of abuses, there is no need for revolution.

Elevated considerations such as these, deeply rooted in the past, seem to inspire the Warren Court's activism. It expresses the conviction that, though freedom may be a dangerous way of life, it is our way. Yet the highly articulate minority led by Justice Harlan is convinced that the majority is headed toward the same precipice from which the Hughes Court, under pressure from Congress, the President, and the country, narrowly saved itself in 1937. But surely the interests and values concerned and the Court's responsibility toward them differ significantly. In 1935–1936, a narrow, headstrong majority, flaunting pleas for judicial self-restraint voiced by a highly esteemed minority, blocked regulation of the economy. In the hands of an obtuse majority, the Constitution became a straitjacket, not a vehicle of life. Confessing the error of their ways, the same Justices, almost overnight, breached the Maginot line they had themselves erected. The Warren Court, on the other hand, in expanding the limits of freedom, in buttressing the moral foundations of society, in keeping open constitutional alternatives to violent change, brings us closer to the ideals we have long professed.

The story, of course, does not end on this note. In certain of the most crucial civil liberties cases, the Justices have split 5 to 4 or 6 to 3. Still facing the Court are issues of great complexity. A living institution, its values, attitudes, and personnel change. Though the Warren Court, on the whole, seems to have achieved the golden mean Chief Justice Marshall thought he had attained, history affords no justification for believing that it will not yet go too far. Justice Harlan, among others, believes that the majority has already exceeded its authority. If so, one may find comfort in the knowledge that our system provides various corrective devices against judicial usurpation. The dramatic repudiation of its own ill-founded precedents, on the heels of Roosevelt's Court-packing threat, contradicts Justice Stone's unrealistic dictum that "the only check upon our own exercise of power is our own sense of self-restraint." Dissenters and malcontents, now as always, alert us to free government's most distinctive aspect—dialogue, conflict, opposition. No opposition means no democracy—no freedom.

Martin Shapiro

THE SUPREME COURT AND FREEDOM OF SPEECH

Now at the University of California, Berkeley, Professor Shapiro is highly regarded for his analyses of the Court's role in the American political process. His book, *Law and Politics in the Supreme Court* (1964) is an excellent argument for this point of view. He has also written, *The Supreme Court and Constitutional Law* (1965), *The Supreme Court and Civil Rights* (1966), and edited *The Supreme Court and Constitutional Rights* (1967), and *The Supreme Court and Public Policy* (1969).

THE ROLE of the Supreme Court, particularly in wielding its power of judicial review—the power to declare statutes unconstitutional—has been the subject of one of the central debates of modern American jurisprudence. The fierceness of that debate is suggested by the difficulty of even labeling the participants without getting caught in the crossfire. One side seizes for itself the labels "judicial modesty" and "judicial self-restraint"—thus suggesting that its opponents are unrestrained and immodest. At the very least they call the other side activists. But would they consent to be called passivists? The "unrestrained, immodest activists," on the other hand, tend to introduce themselves as preservers of a traditional American institution, judicial review, thus leaving their opposite numbers in the unfortunate position of attacking American tradition. But the confusion of labeling is fortunately offset by the appearance of two clear statements by leading members of the opposing schools, Learned Hand, until his death in 1961 one of the America's most distinguished judges, and Professor Charles Black of the Yale Law School. These may serve to focus our examination and clarify the real points at issue.

Judge Hand finds in the Constitution as he sees it a system of separate and coequal departments, each a "Leibnizian monad." Judicial review, which breaches the walls of separation, is contrary to the whole design. Nor does the Constitution provide any specific authorization for review.

. . . [W]hen the Supreme Court invalidates a statute, it perforce substitutes its choice among competing values for that of the legislature. This usurpation will inevitably result in a general recognition of the fact that judges inject their own judicial predilections into law. Once this is realized the principal source of judicial prestige is destroyed, for the real judicial sanction is the notion that courts enunciate the will of the people as expressed in the statutes and the Constitution, not the personal sentiments of the judges.

But Hand's objection to judicial interference with legislative decision does not rest primarily on a judge's self-interest in preserving the judicial myth. It is derived instead from his basic conception of the Constitution and American democracy. The Constitution neither embodies natural law in the sense of an emanation from the Divine Will nor consists of substantive instruction as to the ends of governmental activity. In other words, it is not a code of abstract rights and wrongs but simply a blueprint for the distribution of the people's political power among the several departments of government. Since this plan confides the determination of the substance of governmental policy to the Congress and the President, the only possible role for the Court is to determine whether these departments are operating within the confines established by the blueprint. If the Court attempts to decide whether other departments were "right," a judicial oligarchy "unaccountable to anyone but itself" usurps the task of the "popular assembly" and thus violates "the underlying presuppositions of popular government."

Professor Black's reply to this plea for self-restraint is based on a simple line of logic. The Constitution is law. Courts apply and interpret law. Therefore courts apply and interpret the Constitution. Furthermore, when a statute conflicts with the Constitution, the Supreme Court must decide between the two laws. It cannot avoid the issue for, if one litigant pleads the Constitution and the other a statute, refusal to look to the Constitution in fact decides the case in favor of the statute and against the Constitution. . . .

There are, of course, internal difficulties with the positions of both contestants. Certainly Hand is guilty, at the very least, of overemphasis when he speaks of separation of powers and Leibnizian monads. It is hardly necessary to cite authorities for the proposition that both the relations between the three branches of the federal government and those between the national government and the states have involved a considerable degree of overlapping. Even if we cannot be confident that the framers anticipated such interplay between the geographic divisions of government, the phrase constitutional "checks and balances" serves to remind us that this was precisely their intention for the branches of the national government. Indeed, Judge Hand seems to assign the Court one of the most difficult possible functions when he asks it to set out the boundaries between the various spheres of governmental authority. One can hardly imagine an area more fraught with judicial policy-making than that of jurisdictional surveyor in a governmental system which tends to translate most of its policy questions into disputes over operational boundary lines. . . .

Black wishes to have the best of both possible worlds. His basic argument—that the Constitution is law, that courts deal with law, and that, therefore, the Supreme Court must look to the Constitution—rests on logic. When his rivals poke holes in his logic, he turns to history to demonstrate that his argument has been proved by experience. And when it becomes apparent that the historical picture is not entirely clear, he reverts to his logical argument as a guide to the most reasonable interpretation of history. . . .

All in all, when following the struggles of the champions of modesty and activism, one gets the curious impression that for all the blows and counterblows there is really no solid contact. This impression persists largely because the modest seem to have no very firm position—they roll easily with the punch but cannot deliver a knockout blow themselves. In fact the modest seem to have no more than a set of problems and hesitations which mark a dilemma rather than a solution to the problem of judicial activity. . . .

[T]he Constitution itself, the theory behind it, and the intention of the framers all suggest some sort of judicial review but are neither clear nor decisive about it. The modest are not seeking to ignore or refute the data; indeed, it seems that their modesty is largely derived from a consciousness that the Constitution speaks rather loudly but not very well for review. The problem is not that the activists say that the Constitution requires review and the modest say the Constitution forbids it; it is, rather, that the modest agree with most of the things that activists have to say but, because of the ambiguity of the data, are not totally convinced. The result is not a debate which someone can win, but a running conversation in which one side expresses its self-satisfaction and the other bleats out its doubts.

If the modest experience some tension over the initial authorization for review, they are even more disturbed by the problem of its compatibility with the democratic system. . . . [T]he modest have cautioned that excessive activity by the courts would reduce the responsibility of the people for their own affairs and thus weaken democracy. If the people were to foist many of their governing responsibilities on the courts, they would lose the education by experience which is essential to popular self-government. Because the Congress constitutes the people working out their own salvation through the political process, the Supreme Court must leave it the widest possible responsibility. There is a good deal more to say on this subject and we shall return to it later, but it must be admitted that reliance on the judicial process to the complete exclusion of the rest of the political process would greatly change our system of government. This rationale of the modest does contain at least a kernel of truth. . . .

Thus the modest find that the Constitution is law but not quite the same sort of law as a normal statute, that the intentions of the founders and subsequent history justify review somewhat but not entirely, that the Court and review are neither wholly compatible nor incompatible with majoritarian democracy, and that judicial policy-making is an unavoidable but not completely laudable element of constitutional adjudication. To all this Professor Black replies for the activists that the Constitution is law, that the Court is democratic, that review has the sanction of the founders and of history, and that the Court must make policy decisions. To the modest it can only seem that the activists deal with the dilemma of review by firmly impaling themselves on one of its horns. . . .

If the hosts of the modest are to be delivered from their dilemma, some role and rationale for the Supreme Court must be found which will preserve review but limit it sufficiently, giving it the amount of special justification needed to meet the qualms and suspicions which have been aroused. . . .

We must take a closer look at the "democracy" with which the modest, in revulsion to judicial activism, have armed the "political" branches. . . . Even the most cursory glance at American

politics indicates that Congress and the Executive are not simple, direct bearers of majority sentiment while the Court goes its independent and autocratic way. There are many elements of anti-majoritarianism and irresponsibility in the "political" branches and a rather high degree of responsiveness to popular sentiment in the Supreme Court. In fact, if we must stick to clichéd visions, the most popular and most justified vision today is of Congress as the home of special interests, and the President as the voice of the people—a voice, incidentally, surrounded and often muted by a vast bureaucracy which is itself the home of all sorts of particularistic and partial visions of the public interest.

Now the lawmaker, whom the modest so reverently endow with democracy's banner, is none other than precisely this combination of bureaucracy, President, and Congress, for, quite obviously, all three are major participants in the shaping of our laws. In short, the lawmaker to whom the nasty old undemocratic Supreme Court is supposed to yield so reverently because of his greater democratic virtues is the entire mass of majoritarian-anti-majoritarian, elected-appointed, special interest-general interest, responsible-irresponsible elements that make up American national politics. If we are off on a democratic quest, the dragon begins to look better and better and St. George worse and worse. . . . In fact there are not three branches of government but many centers of decision-making which range from more to less "democratic" and from greater to lesser power, depending on the particular issue involved. . . .

[T]he Court, like other government agencies, can have a clientele. Therefore, two crucial questions emerge in evaluating the political desirability of judicial review. Is the Court contributing to the overall effectiveness of our system of government by representing interests which otherwise would be unrepresented? If so, is the Court's influence strong enough to make that representation worthwhile? On the first issue it has been argued here that the Court's clientele are precisely those interests which find themselves unable to obtain representation from other agencies. There are of course various reasons for this inability. "Potential" interest groups generally lack the impetus for organization because the values they espouse are too amorphous to promote a high rate of personal interaction. Thus, a group built on the value of a tuna fish tariff is likely to enlist a higher degree of immediate political activity than one proclaiming the desirability of fair trial. The tuna fish group is, therefore, much more likely to have available to it the financial and personal resources necessary to gain successful access to a Congressional committee or an executive bureau than is the fair trial group.

The Supreme Court is peculiarly fitted to represent these potential groups. . . .

It is these marginal groups, who champion potential groups and find it impossible to gain access to the "political" branches, which the Court can best serve. Here the modests' dilemma of a Court which is both political and nonpolitical ceases to be a dilemma and becomes a unique contribution to American government. The Court's *proceedings* are judicial; that is, they involve adversary proceedings between two parties viewed as equal individuals. Therefore, marginal groups can expect a much more favorable hearing from the Court than from bodies which, quite correctly, look beyond the individual to the political strength he can bring into the arena. The Court's *powers* are essentially political. Therefore marginal groups can expect of the Court the political support which they cannot find elsewhere. Thus, through a judicial-political court, the potential interest group, via the marginal group, can achieve the political representation which makes a practical reality out of the values it espouses.

Highly organized groups may also turn to the Court, not because they are unsuited to gain access to other agencies, but because, having gained access along with other groups, they lost the political battle. Pressure groups will naturally attempt every governmental avenue which seems promising. If the Court is to make its maximum contribution to the governing process, it should probably devote its major energies to those groups which have little other access to government. It need not act as the last resort of forum shoppers who have been defeated elsewhere. In fact, this desired emphasis seems to accord with the actual power situation, for the Court is capable of major influence precisely when it does represent widespread potential groups, and it can at most offer only minor advantages to organized interest groups which have already failed in their more proper sphere. If the Hughes Court is to be criticized, it is on exactly these grounds: it attempted to make a major intervention against the governing alliance in favor of an organized pressure group which had been defeated in its own customary arena precisely because it was acting contrary to widely held popular sentiment. . . .

[T]he Court exhibits the characteristics of other agencies of government. It is subject to lobbying by a wide range of groups, some of whom find it an essential, others merely a supplementary, source of representation. It will, on occasion, give marginal assistance to nearly any interest. But if it wishes to act effectively in the long run, the Court must reserve its major efforts for its particular clientele.

If the Court is a clientele agency, we would expect it to follow the pattern of other clientele agencies in acting to create and reinforce its own supporting interests. Here the widely held notion that the Court acts as an educator, particularly in the civil rights field, begins to make sense in a political context. Professor Swisher notes that the Court's power "depends on its ability to articulate deep convictions on the part of the people in such a way that the people who might not have been able to articulate themselves will recognize the judicial statement as essentially their own." In other words, the Court's opinions must be designed to bring the widespread sentiments, or as we have put it, certain of the potential groups in society, to the fore. From this strengthened position these groups then support the Court.

Judicial modesty poses a particular threat to this process of interacting support between agency and clientele. For other agencies have learned that they must not only support the values of their supporters, but also tout the particular ability of the agency to serve those values. These two factors become inextricably mixed in agency enunciations, so that it becomes impossible, for instance, to separate the desirability of flood control from the necessity of an active Corps of Engineers. And this is a politically if not logically sound mixture. The strength of the agency, or at least some agency, is essential to the satisfaction of the group interest. Thus the modest opinion, with its praise of the value to be protected and its disavowal of the Court's ability to do the job, is politically suicidal.

The suicide is largely by means of self-fulfilling prophecy. For the more the Court announces its impotence the less group support it receives and the more impotent it becomes. Conversely, the less agency protection the group interest receives the less capable it becomes of politically meaningful action. Thus modest professions of lack of judicial power ignore the real world in which political power comes to those who seek and construct it. We have long since tired of Presidents who proclaim a program but refuse to engage in the cultivation of political support which can make that program a reality. It is time we lost patience with the Justice who proclaims his faith in the value of speech but cannot bring himself to face the political realm in which that value must be protected.

There is something to the argument that the Court must profess some limitations for fear that intervening always and everywhere will result in a dribbling away of its power. Insofar as this means that the Court should not exert itself excessively in the interest of groups on the margins or outside its clientele, it represents sound political counsel. But it must be borne firmly in mind that the building of a clientele is a continuous

process. The Justice who retreats in case after case, husbanding his strength for the really big one, may find when the time comes that he has retreated right off the battlefield. For the Court, like other political instrumentalities, cannot expect to retain its strength without the constant and routine recruiting of support which other politicians call fence mending. The Court has only one means of mending its fences: the opinions it issues. If these opinions do not continuously demonstrate the Court's willingness to act in favor of its supporters, it cannot expect to find much support left when it finally does act.

The concern of the judicially modest has been to differentiate what the Supreme Court might properly do from the legitimate functions of other branches of government. Their difficulty, it seems to me, is that the differentiation has been based on an abstract and artificial view of the American governing process. The Court must indeed attempt to perform its own, not some other institution's, tasks. But what is and is not its own must be determined in the light of actual political arrangements. In that light, the Court can best define its special function as the representation of potential or unorganized interests or values which are unlikely to be represented elsewhere in government.

This approach should release the modest from the dilemma which has led to their hesitancies about judicial activity. That the Constitution is both law and not law is relatively unimportant when judicial review rests not on the question of law and Constitution but on the role of the Court as one clientele agency among many. That review has, and perhaps has not, been historically accepted is less significant than the historical acceptance of a system of national government in which power is fragmented among many agencies including the Court. That the Court is democratic but not entirely so is largely meaningless in a system of government where there are many power-holding institutions, each varying somewhat from the others in the degree of democracy in their selection and their direct responsibility to the people. That the Court deals with law but also with policy is hardly a critical point in a situation where the judicial, administrative, and legislative processes are carried on simultaneously within many of the agencies of government. . . .

In short, the dilemma of majority and special interest, power and responsibility, policy and administration, which the modest discovered when examining the Court, is not so much a dilemma as a set of outer limits within which all American government, not just the Supreme Court, operates. Therefore, that dilemma need not paralyze the Court any more than it paralyzes the rest of the government. More specifically, it need not prevent those interested in freedom of speech from using the Court just as they would any other government agency, particularly when it is one of the means best suited to their purpose. There is no reason why one interest group should deny itself the advantages offered it by a political system which is fully exploited by all other interest groups. A politically realistic assessment of American government leads to the conclusion that neither the defenders of free speech nor the Supreme Court should have any qualms about undertaking as much activity as the current constellation of governmental forces allows them. . . .

IV. NEUTRAL PRINCIPLES OF CONSTITUTIONAL ADJUDICATION v. PURPOSIVE JURISPRUDENCE

The Case for Neutral Decision-Making

Herbert Wechsler

TOWARD NEUTRAL PRINCIPLES OF CONSTITUTIONAL LAW

Herbert Wechsler, Harlan Fiske Stone professor of constitutional law at Columbia, has been both a writer and a practitioner of law in the American political system. His work in the Department of Justice and on many state and federal commissions is well known. In addition, his publications in American Constitutional law, criminal law, and federalism are highly regarded. For example, see *Principles, Politics and Fundamental Law* (1961).

L ET ME begin by stating that I have not the slightest doubt respecting the legitimacy of judicial review, whether the action called in question in a case which otherwise is proper for adjudication is legislative or executive, federal or state. . . .

If courts cannot escape the duty of deciding whether actions of the other branches of the government are consistent with the Constitution, when a case is properly before them in the sense I have attempted to describe, you will not doubt the relevancy and importance of demanding what, if any, are the standards to be followed in interpretation. Are there, indeed, any criteria that both the Supreme Court and those who undertake to praise or to condemn its judgments are morally and intellectually obligated to support? . . . I mean criteria that can be framed and tested as an exercise of reason and not merely as an act of willfulness or will. Even to put the problem is, of course, to raise an issue no less old than our culture. Those

who perceive in law only the element of fiat, in whose conception of the legal cosmos reason has no meaning or no place, will not join gladly in the search for standards of the kind I have in mind. . . .

So too must I anticipate dissent from those more numerous among us who, vouching no philosophy to warranty, frankly or covertly make the test of virtue in interpretation whether its result in the immediate decision seems to hinder or advance the interests or the values they support.

I shall not try to overcome the philosophic doubt that I have mentioned, although to use a phrase that Holmes so often used—"it hits me where I live." That battle must be fought on wider fronts than that of constitutional interpretation; and I do not delude myself that I can qualify for a command, great as is my wish to render service. The man who simply lets his judgment turn on the immediate result may not, however, realize that his position implies that the courts are free to function as a naked power organ, that it is an empty affirmation to regard them, as ambivalently he so often does, as courts of law. If he may know he disapproves of a decision when all he knows is that it has sustained a claim put forward by a labor union or a taxpayer, a Negro or a segregationist, a corporation or a Communist —he acquiesces in the proposition that a man of different sympathy but equal information may no less properly conclude that he approves.

You will not charge me with exaggeration if I say that this type of *ad hoc* evaluation is, as it has always been, the deepest problem of our constitutionalism, not only with respect to judgments of the courts but also in the wider realm in which conflicting constitutional positions have played a part in our politics.

Did not New England challenge the embargo that the South supported on the very ground on which the South was to resist New England's demand for a protective tariff? Was not Jefferson in the Louisiana Purchase forced to rest on an expansive reading of the clauses granting national authority of the very kind that he had steadfastly opposed in his attacks upon the Bank? Can you square his disappointment about Burr's acquittal on the treason charge and his subsequent request for legislation with the attitude toward freedom and repression most enduringly associated with his name? Were the abolitionists who rescued fugitives and were acquitted in defiance of the evidence able to distinguish their view of the compulsion of a law of the United States from that advanced by South Carolina in the ordinance that they despised? . . .

I have cited these examples from the early years of our history since time has bred aloofness that may give them added force. What a wealth of illustration is at hand today! How many of the constitutional attacks upon congressional investigations of suspected Communists have their authors felt obliged to launch against the inquiries respecting the activities of Goldfine or of Hoffa or of others I might name? How often have those who think the Smith Act, as construed, inconsistent with the first amendment made clear that they also stand for constitutional immunity for racial agitators fanning flames of prejudice and discontent? Turning the case around, are those who in relation to the Smith Act see no virtue in distinguishing between advocacy of merely abstract doctrine and advocacy which is planned to instigate unlawful action, equally unable to see virtue in the same distinction in relation, let us say, to advocacy of resistance to the judgments of the courts, especially perhaps to judgments vindicating claims that equal protection of the laws has been denied? I may live a uniquely sheltered life but am I wrong in thinking I discerned in some extremely warm enthusiasts for jury trial a certain diminution of enthusiasm as the issue was presented in the course of the debate in 1957 on the bill to extend federal protection of our civil rights?

All I have said, you may reply, is something no one will deny, that principles are largely instrumental as they are employed in politics, instrumental in relation to results that a controlling sentiment demands at any given time. Politicians recognize this fact of life and are obliged to trim and shape their speech and votes accordingly, unless perchance they are prepared to step aside; and the example that John Quincy Adams set somehow is rarely followed.

That is, indeed, all I have said but I now add that whether you are tolerant, perhaps more tolerant than I, of the *ad hoc* in politics, with principle reduced to a manipulative tool, are you not also ready to agree that something else is called for from the courts? I put it to you that the main constituent of the judicial process is precisely that it must be genuinely principled, resting with respect to every step that is involved in reaching judgment on analysis and reasons quite transcending the immediate result that is achieved. To be sure, the courts decide, or should decide, only the case they have before them. But must they not decide on grounds of adequate neutrality and generality, tested not only by the instant application but by others that the principles imply? Is it not the very essence of judicial method to insist upon attending to such other cases, preferably those involving an opposing interest, in evaluating any principle avowed?

Here too I do not think that I am stating any novel or momentous insight. But now, as Holmes said long ago in speaking of "the unrest which seems to wonder vaguely whether law and order pay," we "need education in the obvious." We need it more particularly now respecting constitutional interpretation, since it has become a commonplace to grant what many for so long denied: that courts in constitutional determinations face issues that are inescapably "political"—political in the third sense that I have used that word—in that they involve a choice among competing values or desires, a choice reflected in the legislative or executive action in question, which the court must either condemn or condone. . . .

But what is crucial, I submit, is not the nature of the question but the nature of the answer that may validly be given by the courts. No legislature or executive is obligated by the nature of its function to support its choice of values by the type of reasoned explanation that I have suggested is intrinsic to judicial action—however much we may admire such a reasoned exposition when we find it in those other realms.

Does not the special duty of the courts to judge by neutral principles addressed to all the issues make it inapposite to contend, as Judge Hand does, that no court can review the legislative choice—by any standard other than a fixed "historical meaning" of constitutional provisions—without becoming "a third legislative chamber"? Is there not, in short, a vital difference between legislative freedom to appraise the gains and losses in projected measures and the kind of principled appraisal, in respect of values that can reasonably be asserted to have constitutional dimension, that alone is in the province of the courts? Does not the difference yield a middle ground between a judicial House of Lords and the abandonment of any limitation on the other branches—a middle ground consisting of judicial action that embodies what are surely the main qualities of law, its generality and its neutrality? This must, it seems to me, have been in Mr. Justice Jackson's mind when in his chapter on the Supreme Court "as a political institution" he wrote in words that I find stirring, "Liberty is not the mere absence of restraint, it is not a spontaneous product of majority rule, it is not achieved merely by lifting underprivileged classes to power, nor is it the inevitable by-product of technological expansion. It is achieved only by a rule of law." Is it not also what Mr. Justice Frankfurter must mean in calling upon judges for "allegiance to nothing except the effort, amid tangled words and limited insights, to find the path through precedent, through policy, through history, to the best judgment that fallible creatures can reach in that most difficult of all tasks: the achievement of justice between man and man, between man and state, through reason called law"? . . .

Let me repeat what I have thus far tried to say. The courts have both the title and the duty when a case is properly before them to review the actions of the other branches in the light of constitutional provisions, even though the action involves value choices, as invariably action does. In doing so, however, they are bound to function otherwise than as a naked power organ; they participate as courts of law. This calls for facing how determinations of this kind can be asserted to have any legal quality. The answer, I suggest, inheres primarily in that they are—or are obliged to be—entirely principled. A principled decision, in the sense I have in mind, is one that rests on reasons with respect to all the issues in the case, reasons that in their generality and their neutrality transcend any immediate result that is involved. When no sufficient reasons of this kind can be assigned for overturning value choices of the other branches of the Government or of a state, those choices must, of course, survive. Otherwise, as Holmes said in his first opinion for the Court, "a constitution, instead of embodying only relatively fundamental rules of right, as generally understood by all English-speaking communities, would become the partisan of a particular set of ethical or economical opinions . . ."

The virtue or demerit of a judgment turns, therefore, entirely on the reasons that support it and their adequacy to maintain any choice of values it decrees, or, it is vital that we add, to maintain the rejection of a claim that any given choice should be decreed. The critic's role, as T. R. Powell showed throughout so many fruitful years, is the sustained, disinterested, merciless examination of the reasons that the courts advance, measured by standards of the kind I have attempted to describe. I wish that more of us today could imitate his dedication to that task.

The Case for Value-Oriented Decision-Making

Arthur S. Miller and Ronald F. Howell

THE MYTH OF NEUTRALITY IN CONSTITUTIONAL ADJUDICATION

Arthur S. Miller, professor of law at George Washington University, has done much work in relating the Constitution to the concept of political values. See, for example, his articles "Notes on the Concept of the Living Constitution" (*George Washington Law Review,* 1963) and, "An Affirmative Thrust to Due Process of Law?" (*George Washington Law Review,* 1962). Ronald F. Howell, now professor of political science at Jacksonville State University, has done similar work, but more from the perspective of political philosophy. His writings cover a wider spectrum of topics from French philosophy to legislative policy-making.

. . . WECHSLER adheres to these ideas: (a) the Supreme Court has a "duty to decide the litigated case . . . in accordance with the law . . ."; (b) the products of the fulfillment of this duty are to be viewed, not as good or bad depending on the result, but in accordance with unstated other standards, these standards presumably to vary from factual situation to factual situation; (c) the Justices on the Court should employ a method which he describes as follows: "the main constituent of the judicial process is precisely that it must be genuinely principled, resting with respect to every step that is involved in reaching judgment on analysis and reasons quite transcending the immediate result that is achieved . . ."; and further: it is "the special duty of the courts to judge by neutral principles addressed to all the issue[s]." Finally, Wechsler tells us that the "virtue or demerit of a judgment turns, therefore, entirely on the reasons that support it and their adequacy to maintain any choice of values it decrees.". . .

On one level . . . are exhortations to members of the Supreme Court to pull up their "judicial socks" and to act more as judges are alleged to act in an idealized view of the Anglo-American system of jurisprudence. This is the level of what can be called superficial or elementary neutrality. It seems to mean at least this: Decisions should be reached in constitutional cases, not in accordance with who the litigants were or with the nature or consequences of the results that flow from the decision, but by the application of known or ascertainable objective standards to the facts of the case. These standards are "neutral" because they have an existence independent of litigants; they are identifiable by Supreme Court Justices (and presumably by lawyers, although none of the . . . authors raises the specter of conflicting neutral principles); and they are usable in making decision and in writing opinions (though it should be said here that the . . . authors are never entirely clear whether it is the results or the opinions explaining those results that they are criticizing). In other words, the collective view of the . . . commentators is one of justice blindfolded, with even-handed application of known principle to known facts. So stated, the position is both an appealing and a familiar one. But it seems to ignore some basic elements of human

Source: Arthur S. Miller and Ronald F. Howell, "The Myth of Neutrality in Constitutional Adjudication," *University of Chicago Law Review,* Vol. 27, No. 4 (1960), pp. 661–691. Footnotes omitted.

activity and, accordingly, has at best only a very limited usefulness. Rather than providing any viable standards for gauging judicial decision-making, it merely restates the question. . . .

The first point we want to make is this: Adherence to neutral principles, in the sense of principles which do not refer to value choices, is impossible in the constitutional adjudicative process. (We limit ourselves to constitutional adjudication at this time, although much of what is said here is applicable to litigation generally.) Strive as he might, no participant in that process can be neutral. Even though this should be thought of as being self-evident, it is desirable to set it out in some detail. Before doing so, however, it should be noted that neutrality of *principle*, as distinguished from neutrality of attitude, is an obviously fallacious way of characterizing the situation. Principles, whatever they might be, are abstractions, and it is the worst sort of anthropomorphism to attribute human characteristics to them. Neutrality, if it means anything, can only refer to the thought processes of identifiable human beings. Principles cannot be neutral or biased or prejudiced or impersonal—obviously. The choices that are made by judges in constitutional cases always involve value consequences, thus making value choice unavoidable. The principles which judges employ in projecting their choices to the future, or in explaining them, must also refer to such value alternatives, if given empirical reference. . . .

[T]he central inferences are clear: (a) choices among values are unavoidable in human knowledge and human activity; and (b) when those choices are made, they are motivated not by neutral principles or objective criteria but by the entire biography and heredity of the individual making them. The wholly disinterested person, be he judge or scholarly observer, does not exist; it can, nevertheless, be said that distinctions may be drawn between decisions in fact made by courts and those recommended by an outside observer who is not a participant in the process.

Professor Wechsler admits that value choices are inevitable, but diverges on the second point of *how* they are made. What we suggest is that his quest for neutrality is fruitless. In the interest-balancing procedure of constitutional adjudication, neutrality has no place, objectivity is achievable only in part, and impartiality is more of an aspiration than a fact—although certainly possible in some degree. In making choices among competing values, the Justices of the Supreme Court are themselves guided by value preferences. Any reference to neutral or impersonal principles is, accordingly, little more than a call for a return to a mechanistic jurisprudence and for a jurisprudence of nondisclosure as well as an attempted denial of the teleological aspects of any decision, wherever made. The members of the high bench have never adhered to a theory of mechanism, whatever their apologists and commentators may have said, in the judicial decision-making process. Even in the often-quoted assertion by Mr. Justice Roberts about the duty of the Court to lay the statute against the Constitution to ascertain if the one squares with the other, one would indeed have to be naive to believe that this statement in fact described the process. Some reference to Supreme Court history will serve to substantiate the point.

Throughout the history of American constitutional development may be found recurring evidence of the fact that Supreme Court Justices have been motivated by value preferences in reaching decisions. At no time have they resorted to neutrality or impersonality of principle in making choices between competing alternatives. Although it is true that from time to time an individual justice has alleged adherence to such a posture—notably Mr. Justice Roberts in his statement in the *Butler* case—the main thread clearly is contrary. The opinions of the members of the Court, particularly those often called the "strong" Justices, such as Chief Justice John Marshall, provide ample evidence of the purposive nature of constitutional adjudication since 1789. The history can be divided into three periods: (a) that to about the time of the Civil War, in which the thrust of Court decision was directed toward forging as strong a national union as law could produce; Chief Justice Marshall is of course the chief exponent of this period and this drive; (b) that from about 1870 to 1937, when the main focus of the Court's decisions was toward providing a favorable climate for business affairs, one free from adverse governmental control; Justice Field early set the tone for this period and the "conservatives" of the 1920's and 1930's embellished it; (c) the post-1937 period, beginning with the constitutional revolution of the 1930's and continuing with the intramural jousting between the Frankfurter and Black wings of the Court. In each of these, it is clear that something far different from neutrality motivated the Justices. . . .

What we wish to emphasize here is that the embattled minority of Justices, who with the flip-flop of 1937 became the majority, were themselves actuated by belief systems no more neutral than their adversaries. One or two of the more celebrated opinions by Mr. Justice Holmes will serve to indicate this. Thus, for example, in enunciating his famous "marketplace" theory of truth in the Gitlow and Abrams cases, Holmes followed what might be called a preference for the theories of the philosophers of the Enlightenment. He stated the classical case for freedom of expression. Thus if the development of substantive due process doctrine in the post-Civil War to Great Depression period of Court history reveals a judicial bias for the economic theories of Adam Smith and [David] Ricardo, so too were the Holmes-Brandeis-Stone series of dissenting opinion illustrative of a set of preferences of those worthies. The question is not whether the Justices during this time followed neutral principles, but rather what value preferences did they espouse.

If that be true in the two periods of time since the Civil War, then it was certainly also true in the pre-Civil War years, particularly those in which Chief Justice John Marshall exercised such a strong controlling hand on the course of Supreme Court decision. Beginning with Marbury v. Madison and continuing for the next several decades, a series of landmark decisions issued from the Court. These had the consequence of forging strong legal chains of national unity, chains which became indissoluble with the civil strife of the 1860's. It is not only the "bad" (by hindsight, at least) decisions, such as those in the Dred Scott case, that illustrated the point. A rundown of the leading constitutional decisions of the first part of the nineteenth century will show as much. Often Marshall seized upon a likely case to write an essay in political economy, sometimes with only incidental relevance to the precise legal issue before the Court. A ready example is McCulloch v. Maryland. And a comparison of the Marshallian method in, say, the Marbury case with that in McCulloch or in Gibbons v. Ogden will indicate that the Chief Justice chose his technique to suit the case at hand. What Marshall started, Taney continued.

The process of non-neutrality continues today and will continue as long as the judiciary is a part of our governmental system. The alleged controversy today over a "preferred freedoms" doctrine clearly demonstrates a conflict in values among members of the present Court, not one of whom can be said to be neutral in attitude. If the "activist" wing of the Court—Black, Douglas, Warren—is quick to speak up for individual liberties and personal freedoms, Frankfurter and the other espousers of judicial self-restraint are also furthering their own set of values. No real need for additional documentation of the point exists. It should, with a moment's reflection, be obvious. . . . It is with particular reference to those peripheral areas, occasioning so much publicity which suggests that American law is in constant flux, that we direct criticism against any theory of allegedly neutral principles. It is precisely in these "new" areas (e.g., national security) that choice must be made among conflicting alternatives. We advocate merely that the value-preferences which determine the choice be stated explicitly. That done, the resulting judgment, were it not for the semantic problem, might even be termed "objective."

In considerable measure Supreme Court Justices themselves are accountable for the recent public image of the judiciary as being everything but objective and neutral. Human nature being what it is, judges who confess that they are not neutral are more readily believed than judges who insist that they are. If the Supreme Court will not first defend its own honor, it is hardly to be expected that anyone outside the Court can do more than take the judges at their word. The issue of judicial neutrality versus judicial interventionism began to be embarrassing in American constitutional law in the 1930's, when the so-called conservatives accused the so-called liberals of judicial malpractice, and vice-versa. Actually the two groups were merely espousing almost opposite judicial values because they subscribed to almost opposite societal values. Far from arguing that judicial values should not reflect societal values, since we believe that they should, we contend only that the American people are entitled at the very least to have those values humbly confessed and assiduously articulated. This the Court did not do in the 1930's or the 1940's or the 1950's. The Sutherland-Stone feud concerning governmental regulation of business has been replaced by the Black-Frankfurter feud concerning the breadth of fourteenth amendment due process. The substantive sphere of conflict has changed, but the procedural feud is still with us. And essentially it is reducible to the lack of consensus on the Court as to the appropriate role of the judiciary in an age in which no national consensus is apparent and no "public philosophy" has yet been enunciated.

The "liberals" of the 1930's and the 1940's could plead piously for the need of "judicial self-restraint" precisely because their battle had already been won, both in the legislatures and in the "public consensus." It is easy, if somewhat sophistical, to insist that the function of the Court is to defer to the legislature in economic matters when the legislature is performing exactly as the Court majority would wish. Yet the liberals applied to their role no such self-restraint in the realm of civil liberties. *That* battle had not been won. Here the Court's rationale was at least convincing, perhaps meritorious; its fundamental premise as to the proper judicial *modus operandi* was clearly expressed: the business of the Supreme Court was primarily the business of civil liberties because the protection of such liberties was the prerequisite of insuring "justice under law" in a free society. . . .

As Justice Holmes earlier seemed most intense when deference to legislative action was posed for judicial advisement, so Justice Murphy later appeared most dedicated to his judicial duty when a civil liberties dispute was being litigated. Other Justices have been most awake when commerce cases were being decided or when the right to privacy and other procedural guarantees were alleged to have been infringed. On the Court at the present time, Justices Black and Douglas are most alert when civil liberties seem endangered. Justices somewhat otherwise inclined look first to the protection of the "national interest" and thus have milder though not less decided views about legislation against subversion and disloyalty. A scholar-Justice like Frankfurter appears primarily committed to quite careful reflection upon any attempt to upset the federal balance.

Finally, in the handling of the facts of a case, again there may be seen the influence of value preferences. That, contrary to popular opinion, facts do not speak for themselves should be axiomatic to any student of the judicial process. The facts of a dispute, as brought forward by the briefs and records as developed in oral argument, and as coming to the attention of the Court by way of judicial notice, are not themselves self-evident propositions requiring no interpretation. They exist only as contemplated by their recipient and are unavoidably colored by the reception given. . . . The point emphasized here is that there are no facts apart from a theory, and that, accordingly, a person's view of the facts is unavoidably colored by the nature of that theory. Neutrality, thus, is unattainable in the constitutional adjudicative process, both on the level of (legal) principle and on the level of the facts of the dispute before the Court. . . .

The role, then, of the Supreme Court in an age of positive government must be that of an active participant in government, assisting in furthering the democratic ideal. Acting at least in part as a "national conscience," the Court should help articulate in broad principle the goals of American society. The process is not a novel one; it has characterized the activities of the Supreme Court in the past, and the suggestion here is that it become outwardly so. Historically, the Court has espoused such goals as the free market, political democracy, and fairness in governmental activities affecting individuals. Today there is an equal need for more conscious normation on the part of the members of the Court. . . .

Hence we suggest that judicial decisions should be gauged by their results and not by either their coincidence with a set of allegedly consistent doctrinal principles or by an impossible reference to neutrality of principles. The effects, that is to say, of a decision should be weighed and the consequences assessed in terms of their social adequacy. Alternatives of choice are to be considered, not so much in terms of who the litigants are or what the issue is, but rather in terms of the realization or non-realization of stated societal values. . . .

V. THE NON-POLITICAL v. THE POLITICAL COURT

The Case Against Judicial Involvement in Political Decisions

John Marshall Harlan

THE BILL OF RIGHTS AND THE CONSTITUTION

John Marshall Harlan was a vigorous dissenter, especially when he served in the Warren Court. He was the grandson of Justice John Harlan who sat on the Court in the late nineteenth and early twentieth centuries and who also was known for his dissents, most especially in *Plessy v. Ferguson.* An oustanding lawyer, the recent Justice Harlan was appointed to the United States Circuit Court of Appeals (2d Circuit) by President Eisenhower in 1954. A year later he was elevated to the Supreme Court, serving until 1971. He succeeded Justice Frankfurter on the Court as the most outspoken proponent of judicial restraint. His argument was that the very structure of American democracy can be endangered by an activist judiciary.

THE MEN who wrote the Constitution recognized, with unmatched political wisdom, that true liberty can rise no higher or be made more secure than the spirit of a people to achieve and maintain it. Their prime concern was to devise a form of government for the new nation under which such a spirit might thrive and find the fullest opportunity for expression. The amendments comprising the Bill of Rights followed only after the structure of government had been established by the Constitution proper. . . . They staked their faith that liberty would prosper in the new nation not primarily upon declarations of individual rights but upon the kind of government the Union was to have. And they determined that in a government of divided powers lay the best promise for realizing the free society it was their object to achieve.

The matter had a double aspect: *first,* the division of governmental authority between the states and the central government; *second,* the distribution of power within the federal establishment itself. The former, doubtless born not so much of political principle as of the necessity for achieving a more perfect union than had proved possible under the Articles of Confederation, was solved by making the authority of the Federal Government supreme within the sphere of powers expressly or impliedly delegated to it and reserving to the states all other powers—a reservation which subsequently found express protection in the Bill of Rights through the provisions of the Tenth Amendment. The second aspect of the governmental structure was solved, purely as a matter of political theory, by distributing the totality of federal power among the leg-

Source: From a speech by John Marshall Harlan reprinted in the *American Bar Association Journal,* Vol. 50 (October 1964).

islative, executive and judicial branches of the government, each having defined functions. Thus eventuated the two great constitutional doctrines of federalism—often inaccurately referred to as the doctrine of states' rights—and separation of powers.

These doctrines lie at the root of our constitutional system. It is manifest that no view of the Bill of Rights or interpretation of any of its provisions which fails to take due account of them can be considered constitutionally sound. The same is true of the due process, equal protection, and privileges and immunities clauses of the Fourteenth Amendment, which, since their adoption following the Civil War, have afforded federal protection against limitation by state action of various basic individual rights. It is an accurate generalization to say that the effect of these two doctrines in combination is to put within the range of federal cognizance only those matters, whether or not denominated civil rights for which a source of federal legislative, executive or judicial competence can fairly be found in the Constitution or its amendments. There is no such thing in our constitu-

tional jurisprudence as a doctrine of civil rights at large, standing independent of other constitutional limitations or giving rise to rights born only out of the personal predilections of judges as to what is good. And it should further be observed that our federalism not only tolerates, but encourages, differences between federal and state protection of individual rights, so long as the differing policies alike are founded in reason and do not run afoul of dictates of fundamental fairness.

It does not derogate from steadfastness to the concept of developing constitutionalism in the field of civil rights —even as we must solve by orderly constitutional processes alone the great question of racial equality before the law —to insist upon *principled* constitutionalism which does not proceed by eroding the true fundamentals of federalism and the separation of powers. To assert the contrary is in effect to urge that the Bill of Rights and cognate amendments to the Constitution be extended so as to become the masters, not the servants, of the principles of government that have served the cause of free society in this country so well.

Alexander M. Bickel

IS THE WARREN COURT TOO "POLITICAL"?

A former clerk to Justice Frankfurter, Alexander M. Bickel, has retained a suspicion of the Court's involvement in political affairs. He is now a professor on the faculty of Yale Law School. His most well-known books are The Least Dangerous Branch (1962), and Politics and the Warren Court (1965); he is also a consistent contributor to The New Republic.

EARL WARREN became Chief Justice of the United States on October 5, 1953 by appointment of President Eisenhower. It was a sudden succes-

sion. Chief Justice Warren's predecessor, Fred M. Vinson of Kentucky, had died unexpectedly that summer, after seven years of service. They were not

Source: *The New York Times Magazine* (September 25, 1966). Copyright © 1966 by The New York Times Company. Reprinted by permission.

years of outstanding achievement. All too often a majority of the Court supported, in a tone of avuncular patriotism, the loyalty-security mania and the xenophobia of the day. In criminal cases, the same majority frequently spoke with the one-sided zeal of the prosecutor. This is, of course, not a comprehensive, and hence not an entirely fair, characterization of the Vinson Court's discharge of its function. For example, the Court also carried forward the process, begun under Chief Justice Hughes in the nineteen-thirties, of desegregating state institutions of higher learning; it declared the white primary unconstitutional, and it forbade enforcement of racial covenants. But these were not the dominant features of the Vinson Court's record.

Earl Warren's tenure as Chief Justice has already exceeded in length that of any of his predecessors appointed in this century. This is, however, the least of the reasons (it is merely symbolic of the fact) that when Chief Justice Warren took his seat in October, thirteen years ago, a new era opened in the history of the Court. Not every decade and not every two decades in the life of that institution constitute an era. And no new era necessarily begins when an old one closes, as one did after the Court-packing fight in 1937. At such a time, it often takes the Court some years to rearrange itself and its doctrines. It takes, Brandeis once said, some years for a new Justice to find himself in the movements of the Court, and it may take the Court some years to find itself in the movements of its time. The current era in the history of the Court dates from October 5, 1953.

As Chief Justice Warren took office, unquestionably the prime business facing him and his colleagues were the school segregation cases. The Court—which then still included Justices Reed, Frankfurter, Jackson, Burton and Minton, in addition to Justices Black, Douglas and Clark, who continue to serve—had heard argument on these cases during the prior term. It had heard the venerable leader of the American Bar, the late John W. Davis, urge that the separate-but-equal rule of *Plessy v. Ferguson* not be reversed. "Sometime to every principle," Mr. Davis had argued, "comes a moment of repose when it has been so often announced, so confidently relied upon, so long continued, that it passes the limits of judicial discretion and disturbance." The Court, before Chief Justice Vinson's death, had then set the cases down for reargument. Mr. Davis's plea had struck a chord, and it is not unlikely that it had struck it in the mind and heart of Chief Justice Vinson, among others.

In no circumstances could a majority of the Court have been found to reaffirm the separate-but-equal rule. But there is reason to believe that had Chief Justice Vinson lived, something very different from the opinion read by Earl Warren on May 17, 1954, would have come down, and something by no means unanimous. The might-have-beens of history are incalculable, and most of them are not significant; the civil rights revolution was coming, in this year or another, by this means and by others, in this institution and in other ones, and it has in any event not been wholly or even mainly the product of Chief Justice Warren's Court. But it would be a foolish determinism which depreciated the importance of the decision of May 17, 1954, and of the shape and manner of that decision.

That was the beginning—and what a beginning: the most consequential judicial event, very probably, in a century—but it was only the beginning. Since then, the Court has declared religious prayer and Bible-reading in public schools unconstitutional; it has ordered the reapportionment of the national House of Representatives and of both houses of state legislatures on an approximate one-man one-vote basis; it has enlarged the rights of the accused in criminal trials; and in decisions culminating just this past term in *Miranda v. Arizona*, it has laid down a whole set of new rules to govern the conduct of police throughout the country toward persons arrested on suspicion of crime. The Court has also—needless to say, this listing is not comprehensive—severely limited the power of government to forbid the use of birth-control devices, to restrict travel, to deny employment to persons whose associations are deemed subversive, and to discourage newspapers, through application of the law of libel, from vigorously adverse comment on the actions of public officials. Finally, without reaching major constitutional issues, the Court has been most niggardly with affirmances of convictions for contempt supposedly committed by witnesses before Congressional committees.

This record is, in all, quite a departure from the records of the Vinson Court, and of its predecessor, the Court presided over by Harlan F. Stone for five years. It is, moreover, in absolute as well as relative terms, a record remarkable for the vigorous exercise of the judicial power, for bringing that power actively and imaginatively to bear on numerous vital issues of the day.

How, then, does one assess such a record? Everything else being equal, it is well for institutions of government to act. But everything else is never equal in a free society, especially in one organized on the principle of federalism. Even in the political organs of the Federal Government, action is not always preferable to forbearance, since there are other institutions, smaller and closer to the people, whose competence should sometimes be respected. And even in those other institutions, action is not always the preferred course, since there ought at times to be a presumption in favor of private ordering. In the Supreme Court, which is the remotest, the most insulated and least responsive of our institutions of government, a rash of decisive action is something of an ominous symptom. It is no sign of healthy progress in our society that so many of its supposed ills should have remained to be cured by the Supreme Court. And yet, the Court has a function, which is not to be performed merely on the periphery of American life. A Court that operates on the periphery, and is otherwise content simply to join a chorus, to speak in the conventional, and as was the case with the Vinson Court, sometimes in the vulgar, tones of a majority of the moment— such a Court does not do its part to make workable the infinite paradoxes of the American system of separation of powers. Such a Court is not the Warren Court. But that is to say very little. It is merely to withhold condemnation.

There are values and interests in play, of course, and it is inevitable that one should judge the Court's actions on segregation, on reapportionment, on school prayers, on criminal procedure, and so on, in accordance with one's system of values and with one's interest. So might one judge the actions of a philosopher king, deeming some good and some bad, and all to be lived with from necessity. But that is clearly unsatisfactory in a democracy, for unlike the subjects of a philosopher king, the people of the United States are not the passive observers of their government, but its masters. They are entitled to know, especially those who do not themselves approve of the Court's actions, why it should have been this particular institution, which they are powerless to control, that took these actions.

No one possesses a systematic and universal prescription for the proper exercise of the Court's role. No one has a self-consistent set of rules that will automatically label one intervention by the Court proper, and another improper. It is a matter of attitudes, of caution and of courage, of vision and of prudence. And it is a matter of history and of tradition, which are certainly not static, and which do not speak with precision to present problems, but which do sanction some and exclude other lines of approach. The Court, like other institutions, is in part the maker of the history and the tradition that bind it, and other institutions are also constrained by the history and the tradition they have made. Unlike the other institutions, however, the Court has no mandate; it is nobody's voice but its own. It is called upon, therefore, to justify its actions in ways not required of the other institutions.

The Court does not discharge its office simply by doing what even most people may think is right or necessary. The Court must be able to demonstrate by reasoned argument why it thought the action right or necessary. It must try to persuade even those whom it may be unable to convince, and to persuade them at least of its own honest and detached effort to apply reason to the problems of society, and to solve them in a manner that is harmonious with a relevant tradition. For if the Court's decisions carry only the authority of its will, what claim have they to control the electoral institutions, and the constituencies of those institutions? If the function of the Court cannot be differentiated from that of Congress and the other political organs, it cannot be justified. The Court is, therefore, not the place for the clean break with the past, not the place for the half-loaf that is better than none, for the split difference and other arbitrary choices, or for the action supported by nothing but rhetoric, sentiment, anger or prejudice.

No one knows how to tell the Court all that it should do and how to do it. It is not so difficult, however, to see what the Court might better not have done, or how it should not have done it. Hence, in addition to those who criticize the Warren Court, as is their right, because they do not like its results, there are professional observers of the Court who criticize it on other grounds, while as a matter of political preference approving many if not most of the results it has reached.

The criticism of the Court that is, perhaps, most frequently heard and that pretty well encompasses all other ones is that the Court is too political. This criticism is misguided or well-taken, depending on what is meant by it. If it means that the Court should make no decisions that can in any sense be deemed political, but should follow some certain body of rules called Constitutional Law, the answer is that The Law as so conceived is a myth, it does not exist, and hence the Court, in order to function at all, must make law rather than simply follow it. Therefore, it must make what are bound to be, in a sense, political decisions.

But if the criticism means that the Court's occasions and modes of policy-making should be different from those of the elected organs of government, then the criticism is well-taken. It means, then, not that this has been a political court but that it has in some instances been wrongly political, that it has been political after the fashion of a legislature or an executive rather than a court.

Illustration of this charge against the Warren Court may begin with the case of *Miranda v. Arizona*, decided this past spring, in which the Court held that police interrogation of a suspect to whom a lawyer has not been made available is in most circumstances unconstitutional. Two years earlier, in *Escobedo v. Illinois*, the Court had foreshadowed this decision. The *Escobedo* case evoked a truly remarkable response. For the first time since the Court had begun to reform criminal procedures, law-enforcement officials themselves set about taking a serious look at what they were doing, and thinking of ways to reform themselves. In addition, the American Law Institute, a private but very prestigious organization of lawyers, judges and law professors, began work on a proposed model code of police procedures.

Had the Court waited another year or two for the fruition of some of these efforts, it could then have decided the final constitutional issues in light of such new procedures as had been worked out. And it might then not have found it necessary to promulgate on its own hook, as in fact it did, a detailed set of rules—a veritable police manual—governing practices of interrogation. The Court might have been in a position, instead, to review rules formulated by others.

Given its insulation, and the inevitably episodic nature of its approach to most problems, the Court is not the suitable agency to make administrative decisions, not the agency to *run* anything. The Court consists of only nine men, each of whom independently considers each case. It must wait for a case before it can act, and in the cases it gets the records and briefs often do not contain all the information and all the ideas that they might. There is little staff, and if there were much more, something would be lost of independent and personal attention to problems by the justices themselves. The jurisdiction is nationwide.

For these, and additional reasons, the Court works best not as a front-line administrator, executive or legislator, not as an initial decision-maker, but as a reviewing agency. There can be, of course, no assurance that other institutions will respond to judicial invitations to take the initiative—*vide* the aftermath as well as the background of the school segregation cases. Yet it makes a difference whether the invitation is issued at all, and whether the Court shows some patience when, as in this instance, the invitation appears to have been taken up.

The Court seemed to know that it was laying itself open to this criticism—to the charge that it was acting more like an administrator or a legislature than a court—since it emphasized in its opinion in the *Miranda* case that the very detailed rules it was laying down for police conduct need not be taken as the final command of the Constitution in every detail. "We encourage Congress and the states," said the Court, "to continue their laudable search for increasingly effective ways of protecting the rights of the individual while promoting efficient enforcement of our criminal laws."

And the Court declared its readiness to be "shown other procedures which are at least as effective" as the ones it was laying down. It remains to be seen, however, whether the Court will in fact be receptive to such other procedures. And it is certain, at any rate, that by seizing the initiative in the *Miranda* case it will have discouraged efforts to work them out.

The *Miranda* case is thus an instance when the Court took on a job that legislatures and other agencies might have been allowed to do first—though this is not to suggest that the job the Court did is altogether a bad one. It is

an instance, in another aspect as well, of a decision that was political in the wrong sense. A week after it handed down its opinion in the *Miranda* case the Court decided that its new rules concerning interrogation of suspects were not to be applied retroactively to convicts now serving sentences. In the past the Court had applied some of its decision in matters of criminal procedure retroactively, and some not. And it had worked out certain reasonably satisfactory distinctions to explain the difference, although of late it had begun to blur these. But the striking thing about the Court's handling of the problem in the *Miranda* situation was its decision not to apply the new rules even in cases quite like the *Miranda* case itself—and there were a few dozen of these pending —in which defendants were appealing convictions that had not yet become final.

Now, the Court may have been justified in declining to risk the general jail delivery that might have resulted from full retroactive application of the *Miranda* rules. A decision to announce those rules exclusively for prospective application, and thus not to apply them even to Ernesto Miranda himself, might also have been supportable. But the rules were applied to Miranda (convicted of kidnapping and rape in Phoenix) and to three additional defendants, and yet not applied to dozens of others in precisely the same situation.

This was arbitrary. It is difficult to think of a rational explanation for it that is consonant with the *Miranda* rules or with rules concerning retroactivity, and the Court really attempted none. And it is in this sense that one may call this action by the Court improperly political, as opposed to judicial. An action for which there is no intellectually coherent explanation may be tolerable, and it may be necessary (it may, for example, be a rough-and-ready compromise that makes possible any action at all), but it is for the political institutions to take, not for the Court.

There are, unfortunately, other illustrations of the sort of decision by arbitrary assertion that in the political institutions is usually the upshot of a series of compromises—or that passes, if you will, for the voice of the sovereign people—but for which there is no excuse in a Court speaking in the name of the Constitution. One such illustration may be found in the famous reapportionment cases of 1964. For in those cases the Court shied away from full adherence to the principle to which its reasoning led—whether that reasoning be thought right or wrong—namely, one man, one vote. The Court has allowed variations from the principle by this or that number of percentage points. The labeling of one variation as constitutional and of another as not is a purely arbitrary exercise, as is the allowance of variations at all.

Again, in the *Ginzburg* obscenity case of last term, finding it all too difficult to articulate a meaningful definition of obscenity, the Court held a book obscene partly for the reason that it was advertised "stimulated the reader to accept [the material] as prurient; he looks for titillation, not for saving intellectual content." The implications of this criterion are far-reaching, and they are staggering. It is highly improbable that the Court intends to pursue these implications and, for example, permit the banning of Boccaccio or Kinsey if improperly advertised. Yet the Court's struggles with the problem have produced no definition of obscenity that would clearly sanction works such as these, while at the same time proscribing Mr. Ginzburg's publication.

But then, what is the basis of the decision? If the Court could find no self-consistent standard to guide it, if, though it groped for a balance between contending interests and ideologies, it found none that it could explain or even seriously promise to apply to other cases in the future, then why should we accept its decision, whatever it may mean? Would we not be much better advised to let the politically responsible institutions strike such balances from time to time without interference from the Court?

Two more examples may be of interest, in which, far from making a prin-cipled decision, the Court seems simply to have settled on that solution of a problem which a majority felt instinctively was about right even if it was not one that could be justified in terms of previously accepted, and as yet unrepudiated, premises. In *Harper v. Virginia Board of Elections* the Court declared the poll tax unconstitutional, holding that it is not plausibly related to "any legitimate state interest in the conduct of elections."

But, complained Justice Black in dissent, "the Court gives no reason. . . ." And it did not. Also dissenting, Justice Harlan argued that payment of a minimal poll tax might plausibly be thought to promote "civic responsibility, weeding out those who do not care enough about public affairs to pay $1.50 or thereabouts a year for the exercise of the franchise." The Court failed even to address itself to this point. And it thus left the impression that it outlawed the poll tax because it does not like it, although as in the rhyme about Dr. Fell, the reason why it could not tell; that is, it could not tell a reason which was persuasive on the premise that, good or bad, qualifications for voting are the business of the states unless they are capricious or based on race.

In *Katzenbach v. Morgan* the Court upheld Section 4(e) of the Voting Rights Act of 1965, which overrides the New York requirement of literacy in English and enfranchises Puerto Ricans literate only in Spanish. The Court supported its decision in part by contending that even if, in the absence of a showing that the vote is denied on the basis of race, Congress has no direct power to change the electoral law of New York, it does have power under the Fourteenth Amendment to cure or forestall other discriminations practiced by the state. Therefore, the Court argued, if Congress thought that Puerto Ricans were otherwise discriminated against by law or administrative action in New York, it had the power to enfranchise them as a means of preventing such discrimination in the future, on the theory that the vote would enable them to protect themselves against discrimination.

But the Court could adduce not a shred of evidence that Puerto Ricans are in fact discriminated against by state action in New York. Furthermore, as in the obscenity cases, the implications of the Court's argument are staggering, and it is not to be assumed that the Court would be willing to pursue them. Yet it simply disregarded them.

The implications are these: presumably, any group which does not have the vote—aliens, commuters from New Jersey, sixteen-year-olds—may be thought to be in danger of being discriminated against by New York in other ways as well; certainly there is at least as much evidence that New York discriminates against aliens and against New Jersey commuters as there is that it discriminates against Puerto Ricans. Consequently, under the Court's reasoning, Congress could bestow the vote on these groups, and on any group which it fears may be discriminated against, even though its fears are grounded solely in the fact that the group in question is deprived of the vote. There is then nothing left of state autonomy in setting qualifications for voting.

The Court, however, did not purport to abolish that autonomy. The opinion, again, is just not intellectually coherent. It upholds the power of Congress to enfranchise Spanish-speaking Puerto Ricans not because on principle Congress ought to have this power but, one must suppose, simply because, like Congress, the Court thought that it was a good thing to enfranchise Spanish-speaking Puerto Ricans, while it would not think it a good thing, perhaps, to enfranchise citizens of New Jersey or aliens.

These criticisms are directed at the manner of the Court's discharge of its function, not necessarily at the results it reaches. They are institutional rather than substantive criticisms, and many people who like the Court's results—and would like them whoever had produced them—have little patience with such criticisms. They want to get on with the business of government and of reform, not theorize about it. But it must be said, with deference, that such

an attitude is very much like being satisfied with Mussolini because he made the trains run on time, or like the late Senator Taft's reported remark that Joseph R. McCarthy, whatever his methods, was good for the Republican party.

An entirely authoritarian government, on the one hand, and on the other hand a government in which all power rests in one or even in a few institutions that are all equally close to the people —either form of government faces few, if any, important institutional problems. It will always be true that some one institution can do some things better than another, and that a wise allocation of competences will take this into account. But the serious problems arise when, as in our system, we distribute some but not all powers to popularly responsive institutions, giving other powers to an authoritarian one, not responsible to the electorate, and when even among the popular institutions some are closer to the people and more readily responsive than others. Then problems of the allocation of competences become serious, because in the end what is in question is democratic responsibility. And so with us the constantly recurring institutional problems are the division of powers between the Federal Government and the states, and the division of powers between the Supreme Court and everybody else.

It is to these problems that the Warren Court, in its spectacular career, has paid less attention than it should. Our system confides to the Supreme Court great power, greater than that of any other judicial body in the world. It is the power to render reasoned, principled decisions. There—in the process by which these decisions are reached, not in the results, however good, humane or politic—is the justification of a power that needs justification in a democratic society, and there also is its limit. And the limit is transgressed—again, regardless of the result—and has on occasion been transgressed by the Warren Court, when a decision is rendered that amounts, after all, to nothing but an arbitrary choice.

Robert H. Jackson

THE SUPREME COURT AS A POLITICAL INSTITUTION

Attorney General under President Roosevelt, Robert H. Jackson was
appointed to the Supreme Court in 1941. He served until 1954, taking a
year's leave at the end of World War II to become chief prosecutor at
the Nuremburg Trials.

FEW ACCUSATIONS against the Supreme Court are made with more heat and answered with less candor than that it makes political decisions. Of course, the line between political science and legal science is not fixed and varies with one's definition of his terms. Any decision that declares the law under which a people must live or which affects the powers of their institutions is in a very real sense political. . . . Of course, it would be nice if there were some authority to make everybody do the things we ought to have done and leave undone the things we ought not to have done. But are the courts the appropriate catch-all into which every such problem should be tossed? One can answer "Yes" if some immediate political purpose overshadows concern for the judicial institution. But in most such cases interference by the Court would take it into matters in which it lacks special competence, let alone machinery of implementation. . . .

The question that the present times put into the minds of thoughtful people is to what extent Supreme Court interpretations of the Constitution will or can preserve the free government of which the Court is a part. A cult of libertarian judicial activists now assails the Court almost as bitterly for renouncing power as the earlier "liberals" once did for assuming too much power. This cult appears to believe that the Court can find in a 4,000-word eighteenth-century document or its nineteenth-century Amendments, or can plausibly supply, some clear bulwark against all dangers and evils that today beset us internally. This assumes that the Court will be the dominant factor in shaping the constitutional practice of the future and can and will maintain, not only equality with the elective branches, but a large measure of supremacy and control over them. I may be biased against this attitude because it is so contrary to the doctrines of the critics of the Court, of whom I was one, at the time of the Roosevelt proposal to reorganize the judiciary. But it seems to me a doctrine wholly incompatible with faith in democracy, and insofar as it encourages a belief that the judges may be left to correct the result of public indifference to issues of liberty in choosing Presidents, Senators, and Representatives, it is a vicious teaching. . . .

It is the maintenance of the constitutional equilibrium between the states and the Federal Government that has brought the most vexatious questions to the Supreme Court. That it was the duty of the Court, within its own constitutional functions, to preserve this balance has been asserted by the Court many times; that the Constitution is vague and ambiguous on this subject is shown by the history preceding our Civil War. It is undeniable that ever since that war ended we have been in a cycle of rapid centralization, and Court opinions have sanctioned a considerable concentration of power in the Federal Government with a corresponding diminution in the authority and prestige of state governments. Indeed, long ago an acute foreign observer declared the

Source: Excerpted by permission of the publishers from pp. 53–83 of Robert H. Jackson, *The Supreme Court in the American System of Government* (Cambridge, Mass.: Harvard University Press). Copyright 1955 by William Eldred Jackson and G. Bowdoin Craighill, Jr., Executors.

United States to be "a nation concealed under the form of a federation." As respected an authority as Charles Evans Hughes declared nearly three decades ago that "far more important to the development of the country, than the decisions holding acts of Congress to be invalid, have been those in which the authority of Congress has been sustained and adequate national power to meet the necessities of a growing country has been found to exist within constitutional limitations."

Here again the principal causes of this concentration have not been within judicial control. Improved methods of transportation and communication; the increasing importance of foreign affairs and of interstate commerce; the absorption of revenue sources by the nation with the consequent appeal by distressed localities directly to Washington for relief and work projects, bypassing the state entirely; the direct election of Senators; and various other factors— all have contributed to move the center of gravity from the state capital to that of the nation.

I think it is a mistake to lump all states' rights together as is done so frequently in political discussions.

There can be no doubt that in the original Constitution the states surrendered to the Federal Government the power to regulate interstate commerce, or commerce among the states. They did so in the light of a disastrous experience in which commerce and prosperity were reduced to the vanishing point by states discriminating against each other through devices of regulation, taxation and exclusion. It is more important today than it was then that we remain one commercial and economic unit and not a collection of parasitic states preying upon each other's commerce. I make no concealment of and offer no apology for my philosophy that the federal interstate commerce power should be strongly supported and that the impingement of the states upon that commerce which moves among them should be restricted to narrow limits.

It was early perceived that to allow the Federal Government to spend money for internal improvements would aggrandize its powers as against those of the states. It was not until the famous decision holding the Social Security Act constitutional that this controversy over the federal power to tax and spend for the general welfare was settled, and settled in favor of the existence of that power in the Federal Government. I believe that this controversy was rightly settled, but there is no denying that the power is vast and, uncontrolled, leads to the invasion of sources of revenue and builds up the Federal Government by creating organizations to make the expenditures. But here we are dealing with powers granted to the Federal Government, if not entirely without ambiguity, at least in language which fairly admits of the construction given it and which fairly warned those who adopted the Constitution that such results might follow.

Considerations of a different nature arise from interferences with states' rights under the vague and ambiguous mandate of the Fourteenth Amendment. The legislative history of that Amendment is not enlightening, and the history of its ratification is not edifying. I shall not go into the controversy as to whether the Fourteenth Amendment, by a process of incorporation or impregnation, directs against the states prohibitions found in the earlier Amendments. Whether it does or not, I think the Fourteenth Amendment has been considerably abused.

For more than half a century the Supreme Court found in the Fourteenth Amendment authority for striking down various social experiments by the states. The history of judicial nullification of state social and economic legislation is too well known to justify repetition here. It came to its culmination when the Court wound up the October 1935 Term by declaring that there was no power in either state or nation to enact a minimum wage law, a position repudiated within a few months by the conventions of both political parties and retracted by the Court itself with some haste. That retraction probably brought an end to the use of the Fourteenth Amendment to prevent experiments by the states with economic and social and labor legislation.

The states have probably been more venturesome and radical in their experimentation than the Congress. This is perhaps explainable by the fact that their experiments are more easily modified if unsuccessful. In the Granger movement and in the social legislation that followed it the states took the lead. On the other hand, they have enacted more extreme legislation for the control and restriction of labor unions when the tide ran the other way. In each instance the interest adversely affected has sought to obtain a holding that due process of law prevented the state from controlling its affairs and also prevented the nation from interfering, thus disabling either from exerting effective control. It is my basic view that whenever any organization or combination of individuals, whether in a corporation, a labor union or other body, obtains such economic or legal advantage that it can control or in effect govern the lives of other people, it is subject to the control of the Government, be it state or federal, for the Government can suffer no rivals in the field of coercion. Liberty requires that coercion be applied to the individual not by other individuals but by the Government after full inquiry into the justification.

Today, however, we have a different application of the Fourteenth Amendment. Today it is being used not to restrain state legislatures but to set aside the acts of state courts, particularly in criminal matters. This practice has proceeded to a point where the federal courts are in acute controversy with the state courts, and the assembled Chief Justices of the state courts have adopted severe resolutions condemning the federal intervention. I must say that I am rather in sympathy with the Chief Justices of the state courts on this subject. I believe we are unjustifiably invading the rights of the states by expanding the constitutional concept of due process to include the idea that the error of a trial court deprives it of "jurisdiction," by including in the concept by interpretation

all other constitutional provisions not literally incorporated in the Fourteenth Amendment, and, in the alternative, by incorporating into it all of our ideas of decency, even to the point of making a constitutional issue of rulings upon evidence.

The Court has been drawing into the federal system more and more control by federal agencies over local police agencies. I have no doubt that the latter are often guilty of serious invasions of individual rights. But there are more fundamental questions involved in the interpretation of the antiquated, cumbersome, and vague civil rights statutes which give the Department of Justice the right to prosecute state officials. . . . I believe that the safeguard of our liberty lies in limiting any national policing or investigative organization, first of all to a small number of strictly federal offenses, and secondly to nonpolitical ones. The fact that we may have confidence in the administration of a federal investigative agency under its existing heads does not mean that it may not revert again to the days when the Department of Justice was headed by men to whom the investigatory power was a weapon to be used for their own purposes.

It is a difficult question and always will remain a debatable question where, in particular instances, federal due process should step into state court proceedings and set them aside. When the state courts render harsh or unconsidered judgments, they invite this power to be used. But I think in the long run the transgressions of liberty by the Federal Government, with its all-powerful organization, are much more to be feared than those of the several states, which have a greater capacity for self-correction. . . .

I know that it is now regarded as more or less provincial and reactionary to cite the Tenth Amendment, which reserves to the states and the people the powers not delegated to the Federal Government. That Amendment is rarely mentioned in judicial opinions, rarely cited in argument. But our forefathers made it a part of the Bill of Rights in order to retain in the localities certain powers and not to allow them to drift into centralized hands. . . .

My philosophy has been and continues to be that [The Supreme Court] cannot and should not try to seize the initiative in shaping the policy of the law, either by constitutional interpretation or by statutory construction. While the line to be drawn between interpretation and legislation is difficult, and numerous dissents turn upon it, there is a limit beyond which the Court incurs the just charge of trying to supersede the law-making branches. Every Justice has been accused of legislating and every one has joined in that accusation of others. When the Court has gone too far, it has provoked reactions which have set back the cause it is designed to advance, and has sometimes called down upon itself severe rebuke.

If an organized society wants the kind of justice that an independent, professional judicial establishment is qualified to administer, our judiciary is certainly a most effective instrument for applying law and justice to individual cases and for cultivating public attitudes which rely upon law and seek justice. But I know of no modern instance in which any judiciary has saved a whole people from the great currents of intolerance, passion, usurpation, and tyranny which have threatened liberty and free institutions. . . .

On the 150th anniversary of the Supreme Court, speaking for the executive branch of the Government as Attorney General, I said to the Justices:

However well the Court and its bar may discharge their tasks, the destiny of this Court is inseparably linked to the fate of our democratic system of representative government. Judicial functions, as we have evolved them, can be discharged only in that kind of society which is willing to submit its conflicts to adjudication and to subordinate power to reason. The future of the Court may depend more upon the competence of the executive and legislative branches of government to solve their problems adequately and in time than upon the merit which is its own.

William H. Rodgers, Jr.

A HOLDING OF "NOT UNCONSTITUTIONAL": LAW REFORM THROUGH JUDICIAL ABSTENTION

William H. Rodgers, Jr., a young writer on the Court, received his law degree from Columbia in 1965. He is currently assistant professor of law at the University of Washington. In this article, he argues that the judiciary has become so involved in political issues that the country will look for guidance from the Court even when it refrains from taking a stand.

IN *Powell v. Texas*, Mr. Justice Marshall held for the Court that the United States Constitution does not prohibit Texas from making public drunkenness a criminal offense. The opinion coincides with the views of the Washington Supreme Court, recently expressed in *Seattle v. Hill*, that the federal constitution does not deprive the states of the power to jail the town drunk as they would a common thief. Many who had relied upon the courts

Source: *Washington Law Review*, Vol. 44 (1969), pp. 607–616.

to forbid the aimless propelling of the "penniless drunk" through the "law's 'revolving door' or arrest, incarceration, release and re-arrest," regarded the decisions in *Hill* and *Powell* with dismay and disappointment. The failure of the judiciary to come to grips with one of society's most persistent and aggravated ills was thought in some quarters to be a betrayal of those who have strived to implement a humane means of treating the chronic alcoholic. It was said that a reform movement, theretofore gaining momentum, had received a serious setback.

These and similar reactions among casual observers of the courts are a common by-product of judicial decisions sustaining statutes against constitutional attack. In recent years, holdings of "not unconstitutional" increasingly have been equated with a judicial endorsement of the policies of the legislation. In the view of many, merely to survive the considerable hazards of judicial review is sufficient to endow a statute with a presumption of wisdom. Especially is this true where the legislation upheld closely resembles similar laws that have been struck down. The current interest of the mass media in judicial decisions appears to have accelerated the trend by transforming the man on the street into an opinionated court critic.

To be sure, the courts, with increasing frequency, are apt to qualify decisions rejecting constitutional claims with a reminder that the legislation sustained may not be the wisest resolution of the underlying problem. But such provisos are likely to go unheeded. Dicta alone will not dissuade the interested public from drawing the inference that the court must have approved of the statute. The popular view is that bad laws will be declared unconstitutional. Lawyers who argue that courts do not strike down statutes indiscriminately because they disapprove of them have difficulty explaining the occasional decisions that resist any other interpretation.

These widely shared attitudes about the consequences and hazards of judicial review have a considerable impact upon the law-making process. Legislation sustained against constitutional attack is likely to serve as a model for similar enactments. Statutes hesitantly enacted acquire an increased legitimacy after successfully withstanding attack in the courts. Moreover, with the rate of attrition as high as it is today, a legislator, councilman, practicing attorney or law professor is loathe to recommend changes that depart substantially from a statute that has survived judicial scrutiny. Only the reckless would jeopardize an enactment by tampering with the model so as to invite further, possibly fatal, constitutional challenges. More pragmatically, problems of drafting are relieved if there is a "good" or "not unconstitutional" draft to draw upon.

Thus the New York statute forbidding the sale of obscene materials to minors, sustained last year, will become the how-to-do it kit for law-making bodies throughout the land. Never mind about other solutions or the limitations implicit in the Supreme Court's reasoning. What is important is that the Court has said that New York's statute is not unconstitutional. Consequently, the political pressures to pass a law just like the one that is not unconstitutional tend to become irresistible.

This phenomenon is gaining momentum and is dangerously circular. The judges, and especially the Justices of the United States Supreme Court, are aware that placing their imprimatur of constitutionality upon a piece of legislation is likely to enshrine it as the recommended solution of a difficult question of public policy. Knowing this, they are increasingly reluctant to legitimate laws offending their own notions of what is just and proper. To be sure, the courts, in an appropriate case, may invoke Mr. Justice Brandeis' techniques of not deciding, of avoiding a decision on the merits of the challenged legislation. The subtle doctrines of standing, ripeness, justiciability and the simple device of construing legislation narrowly, will serve from time to time to postpone decision on difficult constitutional questions. In addition, not every holding of unconstitutionality, for example, on the ground of vagueness or equal protection, will preclude the legislature from tackling the substantive problem by rewriting the statute with greater precision.

But some of the devices for not deciding the ultimate issue of power are currently in disrepute. Opportunities for judicial review have been greatly expanded in recent years by modification of the concepts of standing, mootness and the political question. Avoiding a decision on the merits, moreover, rarely has been a dependable alternative. First, the Congress never has authorized the federal courts to withhold decision in their discretion on difficult questions of constitutional law. In addition, the current preference for presenting a constitutional issue as an abstract question in an action for a declaratory judgment impairs the court's ability to preserve legislation by a limiting construction. And even a decision successfully avoiding the issue may prove to be only a temporary gesture. In practice, given the dimensions of the expanding volume of litigation and the clumsy techniques for avoiding a decision, the judges are incapable, within current jurisdictional limits, of gaining more than a brief respite from the responsibility for deciding the merits of the constitutional issue.

Because courts are reluctant to legitimate an unwise law and unable to defer the decision indefinitely, additional pressures are exerted to strike down more legislation. Lawyers and litigants are eager to resort to judicial review which promises great social reform at minimal cost and exertion. Whoever the proponent, the effort involved in convincing a judge to lift his pen is hardly comparable to the laborious process of drafting a statute and lobbying it through the labyrinths of the legislature or the city council. In *Powell v. Texas*, for example, the premise for the constitutional claim that chronic alcoholism was a defense to the criminal charge was fully spelled out, almost incredibly, in a skimpy twelve pages of testimony by a single expert witness. This submission fell but one vote short of producing an opinion that would have directed a radi-

cal alteration of the treatment of alcoholics throughout the country. With potential rewards such as these no concerned attorney will refrain, nor perhaps should he refrain, from urging that a court render the broadest possible decision on any issue having significant social implications. Few worthy cases will be overlooked because the search for potential constitutional questions is now largely conducted—and the litigation controlled—by organized groups with specific political objectives in mind.

Whatever the reasons for the current popularity of judicial review it is indisputable that recent court decisions have produced an unprecedented growth in federal constitutional law. Alexis de Tocqueville's observation about the nation's early history, that "[h]ardly any question arises in the United States that is not resolved sooner or later into a judicial question," was indeed prophetic. The national judicial authority has been extended rapidly into new domains previously immune from court review. In recent years it has largely supplanted state rules of criminal procedure, evidence, defamation and unfair competition, to name but prime examples. The trend shows few signs of abating.

To summarize, what has been said to this point is that constitutional litigation is becoming a popular pastime. The responsiveness of judges, the erosion of the techniques for not deciding, the easy accessibility of the judicial forum all have combined to bring about increasing reliance upon the courts as the ultimate arbiter of social problems. The question remains whether the drastic expansion of judicial review in recent years has had effects altogether different from what we might expect from an orderly change for the better in judge-made constitutional law.

The law makers response to a holding of "not unconstitutional" points up the problem. Professor Charles Black has argued that court decisions validating governmental action and thus removing constitutional doubt serve a vital role in our society by placing the stamp of legitimacy on dominant political trends. Historically, a conspicuous feature of this legitimating function was to introduce free play into the political process; a judicial affirmation of legislative power could add "impetus and dignity" to tentative law-making endeavors. With a few notable exceptions, however, the broad, sustaining decision, so typical of the Marshall era and even the later days of the New Deal, is becoming a rarity in these days of judicial activism. While the reasons for this phenomenon are many and varied, the sheer volume of constitutional decisions demonstrates that much legislative activity, especially at the state and local level, takes place in a milieu of uncertainty about constitutional power; each new invalidating decision lends further credibility to the threat of judicial intervention. Against this background, when a court chooses to give a statute a stamp of approval; it often imposes a chill upon the legislative process by marking a safe and advisable course for wary political bodies to follow. A legitimating decision, like an invalidating decision, is thus apt to confine rather than reinforce the political elements of our society. As a consequence, we have paid dearly for our new rules of "fundamental" federal law. The price has been a gradual relinquishing of responsibility by the political forces of the community as they dutifully espouse and enact legislation already upheld by the judges.

Preachment about the dangers of excessive reliance upon the institution of judicial review presents no new insights. James Bradley Thayer, at the turn of the century, wrote that when "the correction of legislative mistakes comes from the outside, . . . the people thus lose the political experience, and the moral education and stimulus that comes from fighting out the question in the ordinary way, and correcting their own errors. The tendency of a common and easy resort to this great function [of judicial review], now lamentably too common, is to dwarf the political capacity of the people, and to deaden its sense of moral responsibility." Especially is this true today when the responsible political institutions are coming under heavy fire for their unresponsiveness and impo-

tency. Rusty institutions, long ignored, are likely to become even more unworkable as the ambitious and talented continue to look to the courts for the action. A dangerous misallocation of resources and energies may result as we submit more and more questions to the judiciary in the expectancy that dispositive answers will be forthcoming. The ease and popularity of constitutional litigation suggests that already the skills of many able lawyers are largely destructive; they urge the courts to eliminate bad laws so that a better tomorrow may be built upon the ruins. Too often, however, the struggle subsides after the widely acclaimed constitutional decision is handed down; law revision and bill drafting appear to be unpopular activities. Never mind about rewriting an unconstitutional statute that might be salvaged or especially an unwise statute held "not unconstitutional." Let someone else worry about that.

Excessive reliance upon judicial review not only degrades and debilitates the legislative process but also threatens the dignity and exposes the incapacity of the courts. The Supreme Court's inability to govern the nation, even when it was so disposed, has been demonstrated more than once in our history. Validating and invalidating decisions alike have been proven poor substitutes for political action. Recent experience conforms to this pattern. Indeed, the extension of federal constitutional law, notably through interpretation of the due process and equal protection clauses of the Fourteenth Amendment, has been so rapid and pervasive that an ever-widening gap is discernible between Supreme Court rhetoric and the law as understood and applied in many parts of the country.

The reasons for this are largely attributable to the oft-cited institutional shortcomings of the courts. Subjecting more and more activity to the potential reach of federal judge-made law does not assure effective recognition and implementation of these newly created rights. The influence of an institution, such as the Supreme Court, whose power is largely the power of persuasion and reason, may be wholly nullified if the public supposedly affected by a decision is unpersuaded or uninformed. A court decree unknown to everyone at the operational level—and there are a few—is hardly an effective instrument of social reform.

More pernicious are the instances where the courts' eloquent and forceful declarations are clearly perceived by the public at large and yet unheeded in the political arena or ignored by the administrative process. The evidence of a growing disparity between the written decisions and the law observed by those who daily come into contact with the legal system is becoming ominous although perhaps inevitable in light of the recent and vast doctrinal development. To many the school desegregation decisions have been an empty promise; they will remain so until forces stronger than judicial reason take up the cause. Miranda has had little real impact on police practices. Prayers are still in style in many of the nation's school rooms. The examples could be further multiplied. The important point is that in a number of cases for different reasons the courts' sweeping affirmation of principle may prove to be largely unrealized and unrealizable. Judicial rhetoric promises more than it produces; practice lags further behind declared constitutional principle. Yet the demand for more rhetoric is continuing unabated.

This is not to say that the courts should cease declaring constitutional principles because they cannot assure universal enforcement of those principles. It is to say, however, that the role of the judiciary in a rapidly changing and complex society requires a continuing reevaluation. Political officials, both law-makers and law-implementers, as well as the judges themselves, must be alert to forces in the community that constantly redefine their respective problem-solving capabilities. De Tocqueville wrote for a different day when he said that social problems in America necessarily become translated into judicial problems. Holmes, as well, did not speak to our present social dilemmas when he described law as a simple prophecy of

what the courts will do in fact. What the courts will do and what the courts can do effectively are different questions.

Too often we forget that the judges have neither the time, the resources, the capacity, nor the political responsibility to resolve many of the issues thrust upon them. These institutional deficiencies are more pronounced as debatable issues of social policy implicate the concerns of more people and radiate broader controversies. It is sufficient to suggest that we must rid ourselves of the notion, unfortunately too prevalent, that the complex social problems that beset modern America may be stilled by an occasional word from an appellate bench; knotty questions of race relations, poverty, population explosion and environmental contamination hardly will be litigated into oblivion. Meaningful law, law that will be felt in day-to-day human conduct, can only be shaped by aggressive and widespread social, political and administrative action. We delude ourselves when we attempt to shunt this responsibility onto the courts.

The judges, too, should remain acutely aware of their limited constitutional role. Marbury v. Madison, after all, did not impose upon the judiciary a special license to pass judgment upon the wisdom of statutes. Unlike the legislators, judges are locked into a decision-making discipline by the language of the document being construed and by considerations of history, precedent and reason. Sitting as courts of law, they have a special responsibility to reach a judgment "on analysis and reasons quite transcending the immediate result that is achieved." Part of this reasoning process requires an awareness that courts are simply incapable of declaring and supervising the effective implementation of many choices of social policy; and that insuperable administrative difficulties might justify caution in proclaiming unrealizable constitutional principles.

Perpetuation of a wide gap between judicially-declared principle and actual practice becomes, in the long run, outright hypocrisy. By validating legislative or administrative action the courts may avoid the accusation that they are making false promises that cannot be fulfilled. More important, a sustaining decision leaves the responsibility where it should be and in the long run must remain—namely, with the political process. From these premises it follows that a holding of "not unconstitutional" is far removed from the popular view that the legislature's resolution of the problem was in full accord with the better wisdom of the times. Calling a statute "not unconstitutional" is, as the wag observed, very much like saying a woman is "not ugly." Whether she is also beautiful turns on circumstances beyond the court's control.

Suffice it to say that the notion that the judges must solve all our problems, and indeed deserve to be condemned for not doing so, should be banished. The judicial power, never an effective instru-ment of social reform, is all the more inadequate in the face of today's enormous social problems. A holding of "not unconstitutional" simply confesses this inadequacy. The fundamental lesson to be learned from *Powell v. Texas* is not that the Supreme Court applauded the practice of treating drunks like criminals. It said, rather, that concerned people who are interested in attacking the problem will find no easy solution in the courts. No reform movement has been squelched, no principles betrayed. A Supreme Court decision, whatever it declared, could not have transformed a jail's drunk tank into a hospital's detoxification center. The work remains to be completed, in the State of Washington and elsewhere, by those who are capable and willing to shoulder the burden of political action.

The Case for Judicial Involvement in Political Decisions

Laurent B. Frantz

THE FIRST AMENDMENT IN THE BALANCE

Laurent B. Frantz, now editor of the Bancroft-Whitney Publishing Company, served briefly on the Faculty of Drake University Law School. In addition to this piece, he has contributed to other publications in the field of constitutional law.

. . . AN ECONOMIC mistake or injustice does not interfere with the political process and that process therefore remains open for its correction or redress if the courts refuse relief. The same cannot be said where legislation results in infringement of political rights, for the injured can hardly rely for redress on the very weapons of which they are deprived. Even Mr. Justice Frankfurter has recognized that this distinction justifies two different standards of judicial review. Furthermore, economic interests are typically represented in legislative bodies—or able to obtain a hearing from them. Despised ideological minorities typically are not. In extreme situations such as those which give rise to first amendment test cases, their political influence may be less than zero, for it may be better politics for a legislator to abuse them than to listen to their grievances.

Under such circumstances, judicial deference to a legislative judgment curbing the political rights of a minority is hardly the same "judicial restraint" espoused by Justices Holmes and Brandeis, which allows considerable latitude to legislative judgments on the need for economic reform.

"Activism" in economic review narrows the range of popular choice by prescribing that there are certain legislative experiments which may not be attempted. "Activism" in libertarian review prevents a narrowing of the range of popular choice by preventing Congress from circumscribing that area of permissible discussion and advocacy which is the ultimate source of social change and legislative innovation. The historical evidence, far from suggesting that the two go together, indicates that they have always tended to be mutually exclusive.

But the advocate of "judicial restraint" will insist that where there is room for a reasonable difference of opinion between Congress and the Court as to whether certain action violates the first amendment, Congress' view should take precedence. There are excellent reasons why it should not. First of all, "Congress shall make no law . . ." is an obvious and express effort to restrain congressional power. If that restraint is to be effective, then Congress is the least appropriate body in the world to be accorded the final word as to what it means. And, while I have no desire to re-wage the general battle for judicial review, the evidence is reasonably clear that the first amendment was proposed with the express expectation and intention that the courts would enforce it.

When a bill which is dubious on first amendment grounds is proposed in our

Source: *The Yale Law Journal*, Vol. 71, p. 1424. Reprinted by permission of the Yale Law Journal Company and Fred B. Ruthman & Company.

Congress, Congress may debate its constitutionality—but it does so on the implicit, and often explicit, assumption that anything which the courts will permit is constitutional. And it appears to feel no impropriety in treating constitutionality as a mere technical obstacle which may, perhaps, be avoided by astute draftsmanship. If the statute is enacted and the courts uphold it by deferring to the legislative judgment, they are deferring to a judgment which, so far as constitutionality is concerned, has never really been exercised.

Furthermore, this argument for "judicial restraint" takes no cognizance of an important feature of our system: judicial enforcement of a challenged statute is not abstention, but validation. So far as constitutional power to enact it is concerned, it is an endorsement of constitutionality by the body still recognized as having the final word on the subject. Whether that result is reached on constitutional or pragmatic grounds, or merely by deferring to the legislative judgment, it becomes a constitutional precedent which Congress can rely and enlarge upon in the future.

Perhaps Congress should take more responsibility for constitutionality. And there may be ways, even within our present system, by which that responsibility can be increased, but judicial rubber-stamping of anything which Congress at a particular moment may reasonably think desirable is not one of them.

Charles L. Black, Jr.

THE CHECKING WORK OF JUDICIAL REVIEW

Charles L. Black, Jr., is the Henry R. Luce professor of jurisprudence at Yale. He is an articulate and enthusiastic defender of judicial activism, and he does not fear to take the offensive against those espousing judicial restraint. Besides his works in law such as *Perspectives in Constitutional Law* (1963), he has also had a book of verse published.

. . . [I]N CONTENDING that judicial review has a valuable negative function, one that should be exercised in appropriate cases with vigor and without apology, I am toiling uphill against that heaviest of all argumentative weights— the weight of a slogan. The slogan . . . is . . . "judicial restraint." Whenever the possibility arises that the Supreme Court might act with decisiveness to implement any of the guarantees written into the Constitution, this slogan is wheeled again into the breach and made to serve yet once more. And it has had a marvelous (and in my view a baleful) efficacy in inhibiting even a prudently restrained use of the judicial power to give effect to the deeper policies of our basic law. It has become the universal hypnotic and tranquilizer, the one sluggish lodestone of wisdom, the all-sufficient clew-thread for judicial activity, or, rather, inactivity. It has catalyzed scholars and judges to phrenetic search for theory after theory, technicality after fine-drawn technicality, on the basis of which the Court could in the pending case escape clear-cut action, and refer the duty of decision to another department or to the Void.

Perhaps it is not after all so marvelous that this slogan should have enjoyed the vogue it has. Its phrasing, though pithy, is a work of art. Nobody feels quite easy in coming out against "restraint," any more than against a "right-to-work" law, or "fair trade." "Judicial timidity" or "judicial buck-passing" would have less appeal, though the facts referred to might often be quite as naturally described in the one way as in the other. If you promulgated and popularized the concept of "military restraint," you might have some trouble getting a battle fought when it needed to be fought; the parallel, indeed, is not fanciful. And the concept of "restraint" sits with particular appropriateness next to the concept "judicial"; one of our archetypes of the judge is a figure listening without excitement and acting very slowly, and it is easy to confuse this picture with that of a judge listening without passion for justice, and determined not to act at all.

Nor is the appeal of this slogan the result of mere popular or academic perversity. It embodies, as a slogan is likely to do, just half of the truth. Half of the truth is something. Though it may not always satisfy the proverb concerning half a loaf, it may be worth keeping around until we find the other half. But half of the truth bleeds at the torn edge. Restraint in prudent measure, deference to the other branches of government, painstaking attention to the limits of judicial jurisdiction—these things we look for in our judges. But we look, and ought to look, for something else—a strong, clear, definite acceptance of the final responsibility for decision on matters of law, and the intellectual courage to exercise that responsibility in actual practice and without resort to cobweb subtleties excusing evasion. Our Court was never put where it sits, not only in the tangible government but in the great image of government that is in the hearts of our people, for the sole purpose of devising reasons (as reasons always can be devised) for evading the firm decision of great constitutional questions.

You may say that the line between prudent restraint and courageous decisiveness is hard to draw. Of course it is hard to draw; it is impossible to draw with anything like concise logical precision. In this it resembles the line between not eating enough and eating too much. The essential thing to keep in mind is that sickness and even death inhere *both* in malnutrition and in obesity. The sloganeers of judicial restraint see only one danger. They are like the man in Chesterton who loved (as who could not) the noble color red, and who proceeded to paint the town—houses, lampposts, and all—uniformly with this color. "Judicial restraint," they say, "is good; let us therefore have as much of it as possible. Let us paper the universe of constitutional law with the leaves of articles and books and opinions that spin out carefully contrived reasons for the Court's remitting the task of decision to somebody else, and before you know it we'll have enough reasons to cover every possible case."

This attitude is very old in America, but its vogue is relatively recent—a matter of the last few decades, with a full florescence going scarcely farther back than ten years. It represents, I think, an overreaction to certain judicial excesses of an earlier time; it is a mechanism of defense against a danger which no longer looms, though it may lurk . . .

Now it is entirely consonant with the theory of judicial review for the Court to take the position that great deference is to be paid to the judgment of Congress as to the extent of the powers affirmatively granted to itself. This need not be placed on a mystique of judicial restraint; it can rest on grounds of sound substantive constitutional interpretation. It is quite reasonable to suppose that the body that is given the power to tax "for the general welfare" was intended to be given the power to determine, within wide limits, wherein the "general welfare" actually consists. The power to "raise and support armies," on a reasonable construction, contains a wide discretion to determine what an army may appropriately comprise under the military circumstances of the time, and what steps are requisite to its recruitment and maintenance. It is a more than reasonable supposition that the power to enact laws "necessary and proper" to the carrying out of the objectives of government imports an ample latitude of decision as to necessity and propriety. "Judicial restraint" in such cases may be taken as a mere shorthand term, expressing the philosophy of broad construction of the language granting power to Congress. No special or separate philosophy of "restraint" is required to reach the truistic conclusion that the Court ought not to strike down a statute as exceeding Congressional power when in the judgment of the Court the statute is within the limits of Congressional power. If the Court is inclined to broad construction of the constitutional grants of power, then it cannot and ought not very often find itself invalidating statutes on this ground. All who approve of broad and flexible constitutional construction can approve of this scarcity of judicial checking of Congress, without any necessary reference to a general concept of "judicial restraint."

I would begin the affirmative case for vigorous judicial enforcement of the Bill of Rights guarantees by pointing again to the fact that they are *prohibitions.* They were meant to limit government, and the consequence of their judicial enforcement is that they do limit government. This point, as near truism as it is, needs to be made. For the constantly reiterated theme of the monotheistic idolaters of "judicial restraint" is the utter unfitness, the radical disconsonance with our theory of government, of there being set any limits to the popular will as expressed in elections. Article I, Section 9, and the Bill of Rights, contradict and finally disaffirm, where all may see and with the clarity of bright sunshine, the theory that the entire exemption of government from limitation is an authentic part of the foundations of our polity. . . .

If the Court is charged with enforcing the Bill of Rights, even against actions of Congress, then the conclusion that the invoked guarantees are to be broadly construed leaves no alternative to vigor-

ous, vigilant, courageous activism on the part of the Court in applying them. Those to whom "judicial activism" is a naughty expression do not want to be placed in the position of contending for narrow construction of the Bill of Rights —and (such are the powers of compartmentation in the human mind) it must be said in fairness that many of these people do not actually favor such a construction, though the consequences of their position are the same as those of the view that would blandly construe the Bill of Rights away. Consequently, they attack at the other possible point, contending, in effect, that the Court has no business interpreting and applying the Bill of Rights, or some of it, but ought to leave the question of its construction up to Congress. And by and large they call for the Court to abdicate, either forthrightly or by a set of euphemisms, its position as final and effective authority on the meaning of this part of the Constitution. These people have had some success, but they have not yet won an irreversible victory.

There is an amazing paradox in this position. For the people who espouse or insinuate it support their view, in the main, on the ground that the interpretation of the Bill of Rights requires the making of judgments of *policy,* and that it is unsuitable for a court to make such judgments. Their attack, in this respect, is a part of a broad offensive against judicial review as a whole, . . . The paradox arises from two facets of the matter. First these people are asking for what amounts to a Constitutional amendment of the very first magnitude. They are asking that the Court remove itself in fact from the performance of a function which the great majority of American political thinkers from the beginning to now have assumed it was to perform, from a function in which it has been repeatedly confirmed by statute and by the authoritative concession of the other departments. They are asking the Court to decline, in effect, to do a job which is constitutionally committed to it just as firmly as history could have committed it. They are asking the Court to falsify every high-school civics teacher who ever laid out the cut-and-dried, un-debated facts about American govern-ment and about the place of the Court in its operation. They are asking that this be done by a series of judicial ab-stentions and deferrings to Congress, but this cannot conceal the fact that the Court that did it would be perpetrating one of the boldest acts of judicial legis-lation in history, an act that, as soon as it was recognized for what it was, would change the whole form of our govern-ment. Secondly (and here is the para-dox) they are asking that this be done simply and solely on grounds of policy! They have thought over the policy of the thing and have come to the conclusion, on prudential considerations that seem good to them, that it is not well for the Court to exercise this function which Holmes and Brandeis and Taft and Hughes all thought it had. The consid-erations that are put forward have to do with the suitability, as a *sheer matter of policy*, of the Court's exercising the power of invalidating statutes which it considers to violate the Bill of Rights. These deplorers of the intrusion of policy factors into judicial judgment, these insisters that the Court must remit all questions of policy to Congress, are asking that the members of the Court, on pure policy grounds, reverse the un-ambiguous constitutional assumptions of a century and a half, and decline, on these grounds, to perform a role which virtually every thinker, deep and shal-low, has always conceded to be theirs—and in which Congress itself has con-firmed them. In brief, they are asking the Court to decide to give up its role as interpreter of the Bill of Rights, on the sole ground that it is bad policy for judges to decide policy questions! . . .

Surely it is not the place of the Court to abdicate this role because it thinks someone else could play it better, any more than it is the place of the President to stop appointing judges because he thinks it would be wise for them to be elected. But the people and Congress always have in their hands the means (not only through Constitutional amend-ment but through the abundant power of Congress over the jurisdiction of all the federal courts) either to remove the Court from the function of guarding the Bill of Rights, or so to embarrass it in the exercise of this function as to make its work of little practical value. And the nuances of the judicial process are such that, if it ever came to be settled professional dogma that it was a great historic mistake to commit to the courts the responsibility of refusing to give effect to laws which in their judgment infringed the Bill of Rights, the effect on judicial resolution in the vigorous per-formance of this task would inevitably be great. Hence it is well to ask the further question: Is it a sound plan to continue to refer the decision of these questions to the Court, rather than so arranging matters (by any device from Constitutional amendment to judicial sophistry) that the judgment of Con-gress shall be practically final?

The usual argument to the contrary rests on the suggestion that interpreta-tion of the guarantees of the Bill of Rights ought to be exclusively commit-ted to the "political process." This for-mula contains almost too much irony to be taken wholly seriously. Those who need the Bill of Rights need it because they cannot prevail in the "political process," in the sense in which the latter term is used by those who put this thought forward. Those who wrote these guarantees into the Constitution must have known this; what other conceiv-able reason is there for placing consti-tutional prohibitions on Congress? In many cases, moreover, the wrong com-plained of is one that amounts to an exclusion from the "political process"—such as suppression of the voicing of political opinion. But in virtually all cases the interest shielded is a minority interest, and often one that is intensely unpopular. To remit such people to the "political process" is only a shade less hilarious than to suggest (and some have actually suggested this!) that the Ne-groes of the South ought to be remitted to the "political process" for protection of their rights—including, one pre-sumes, the right to vote!

. . . In this broader and more accurate sense, it is meaningless to contrast the "judicial" and the "political" processes; if a man were to voice a view forbidden expression by Congress, and if the Court declined to send him to prison on the ground that Congress was itself forbidden by the First Amendment to make such a law, that man would have been freed by the "political process," in this deeper sense, just as surely as if he had been granted an amnesty by the vote of both Houses of Congress.

Here we touch, I think, on the edge of another paradox, and this one, it seems to me, opens out on endlessly creative horizons. Those who would do away with judicial review, whether by overthrow or by erosion, often base their position on trust in the people, with the implication that trust in the people forbids judicial interference with the people's determinations. But I think they miss the most important reason for trusting the American people, and it is a reason which vitiates their whole argument. The American people are trustworthy above all because they possess the quality without which no one is worthy of trust. They can be trusted, because they do not trust themselves. . . .

We come back around to the slogan with which we began . . . "judicial restraint." I have tried to counter this slogan with a concept—which I have not the art to sloganize—of a very different kind of restraint. I mean the restraint of the people by themselves—the self-restraint of democracy.

For that is what judicial review amounts to, in its negative aspect. It is presented conventionally as a contradiction to popular government, as an exotic in the clime of democracy. But after all it can hardly be that; how would it have survived? It has survived because the people wanted it to survive; it could have survived on no other terms.

Our government was founded and accepted by the people on the condition that its powers be limited by certain prohibitions. The people have accepted, to say the least, the principle that these limitations are to be given effect in court by judges. Neither the limitations nor the means of enforcing them could have lasted any five years if the people had not wanted them to last. How curious a misreading, to see in these institutions a contradiction to popular rule! They embody the most impressive kind of popular rule—self-rule. Other nations have other means of self-rule—of doing the work for the nation as a whole that temperance and forethought and forbearance do for the sane individual. Judicial review is one of our means to this end—doubtless, if one throws in its ritualism and symbolism, our chief means. . . .

Loren P. Beth

THE SUPREME COURT AND STATE CIVIL LIBERTIES

Loren P. Beth is professor of government at the University of Massachusetts. Author of *Politics, the Constitution, and the Supreme Court,* Beth disputes the restraintists' concern with federalism. Instead, he argues that as far as constitutional rights are concerned, there should be no difference between the federal and the state governments.

ONE of the major themes in recent writings about the United States Supreme Court has been its treatment of civil liberties cases. During Chief Justice Vinson's tenure much comment, pro and con, was elicited by the Court's comparatively "restraintist" approach to such cases. And in the years of Chief Justice Warren, as the Court has become more "activist," the same writers have labored the same themes, but with the pros and the cons reversed. The attitudes and voting records of individual justices have been closely scanned to see whether they "measured up" to the standards of the investigator; "box scores" have been compiled purporting to show such attitudes; particular justices have had their attackers and defenders—and more than one sitting judge has doffed his judicial halo long enough to defend himself (sometimes more effectively than his admirers).

The present writer has been among those who have attacked the Vinson court and defended the Warren court; and with the judges and other writers he has been accused of fostering the same approach to civil liberties which did the Court so much harm when it was used in the economic sphere before 1937. But such charges have been often denied, and the modern-day "activists" are seemingly fairly well convinced that they have built up a rationale to distinguish the two types of cases which is convincing (at least to themselves): they no longer have guilt feelings about their own inconsistency on this score.

There is, however, another question with which the defenders of activism in civil liberties have not dealt effectively as yet. This is the question involving the Fourteenth Amendment. After all, say the critics, even if you prove that the Bill of Rights should be industriously applied by the Court, the fact remains that the first eight amendments apply only to federal action; and while the due process clause of the Fourteenth Amendment has been used to extend parts of the Bill of Rights to the states, this process is really illegitimate because the clause does not logically bear such interpretation and because this amounts to the use of the now-discredited substantive interpretation of the clause. So another inconsistency is charged against the libertarians. The present article is an attempt to investigate such criticism and lay the groundwork (if possible) for a defense. Put simply, the question is: can the Supreme Court justify the use of the Fourteenth Amendment to apply the Bill of Rights as against state action? (The assumption throughout is that the Court *can* do so as against federal action: those who question this are invited to look elsewhere for its justification.)

This question is important because of the known fact that the threat to civil liberty has, in America, most often been a *state* threat. The reasons for this will be further investigated later in this paper, but the fact can hardly be gainsaid. After all, it was Mr. Justice Holmes who wrote (in his usual quotable vein),

Source: *Western Political Quarterly,* Vol. 15, No. 4 (December 1961). Reprinted by permission of the University of Utah, copyright holder.

"I do not think the United States would come to an end if we lost our power to declare an act of Congress void. I do not think the Union would be imperiled if we could not make that declaration as to the laws of the several states." It is probable that Holmes had in mind the preservation of the federal system rather than the protection of civil liberties, but his statement is equally applicable to the latter. If civil liberties can benefit from judicial protection, that protection will be of most importance where state infringements are concerned. The very multiplicity of state and local governmental units would account for this; but the facts of their political lives redouble the effects. As Bernard Schwartz has pointed out, "from the point of view of the average American citizen, the danger of abridgement of his civil rights arises largely on the level of State or local government."

THE MEANING OF THE FOURTEENTH AMENDMENT

There have been several book-length studies of the Fourteenth Amendment published in the last dozen years, in addition to many shorter articles. The recent interest in the Amendment has been stimulated in general by the Court's activities in the civil liberties field, but it was probably touched off by Justice Black's somewhat rash conclusion in his *Adamson* dissent that its framers intended to include the whole Bill of Rights in the first section of the Amendment. Fairman and Morrison have written at length to disprove Black's thesis; they have at least succeeded in indicating that the Justice erred in basing his conclusions on insufficient scholarly study if not in the conclusion itself. . . .

The broadest view of the coverage of the Amendment has been taken by Joseph B. James and Jacobus tenBroek. James has written the most complete blow-by-blow account of the legislative process by which it was adopted, while tenBroek has investigated the theories of the abolitionist movement (assuming the Amendment to be the culmination of that movement). Both writers conclude that while the Amendment may not be a specific application of the Bill of Rights to the states, it is in fact something even broader: the natural rights of man whether or not contained in written constitutions. James writes that "it is not too much to say that the existence of a federal Bill of Rights in written form was entirely unnecessary for the purposes of the Fourteenth Amendment." And tenBroek concludes, "the rights sought to be protected were mens' natural rights, some of which are mentioned in the first eight amendments and some of which are not." Both writers refuse to view the three major clauses of the amendment as separate and exclusive; they are instead "mostly but not entirely duplicatory."

A second theory is that the Amendment was intended to apply the federal Constitution's Bill of Rights to the states. Despite certain ambiguities this seems to be what the first Justice Harlan had in mind in his dissenting opinion in *Hurtado v. California*, in which he said that the Fourteenth Amendment "evinces a purpose to impose upon the states the same restrictions, in respect of proceedings involving life, liberty and property, which had been imposed upon the general government." While this seems to depend on the due process clause alone, his fuller statement in *Maxwell v. Dow* seems to base it on the Amendment as a whole. Justice Black's famous dissent in *Adamson v. California* expresses the same idea: "The original purpose of the Fourteenth Amendment" was to "extend to all the people of the nation the complete protection of the Bill of Rights." . . . These views, however, have been uniformly rejected by Court majorities.

Turning to more restrictive ideas of the Amendment's meaning, Professors Fairman and Morrison, after exhaustive investigation, conclude that the Bill of Rights is obviously *not* included in the Amendment; but they concede that there is some basis for believing that some parts of it—particularly the First Amendment—may be incorporated in the privileges or immunities clause. Professor Lien arrives at much the same conclusion. Except for a significant shift in clauses, this has been the dominant Court view since (at least) Justice Cardozo's opinion in the Palko case. In that case the Court granted that certain of the provisions of the Bill of Rights (or, more precisely, the rights contained in such provisions) may be said to be imported into the Fourteenth Amendment, but through the due process rather than the privileges or immunities clause. The difference may seem of slight importance; but since the use of the due process clause requires much the same kind of substantive interpretation which (when applied to economic matters) involved the Court in so much trouble in the period from 1895 to 1937, many people dislike using it. . . .

Until the 1920's the Court was not much interested in civil liberties; and by the time it became so, the due process clause—already expanded to meet the exigencies of corporate enterprise—was ready to hand, which made it unnecessary to resurrect the privileges or immunities clause. . . .

One should keep in mind not only the representative qualities of state governments but their propensities as well. It is all very well to speak glibly of allowing "experiments" in the "insulated compartments" provided by the federal system. But it should not be forgotten that these experiments, even though confined to one state's territory, affect the lives and freedoms of multitudes of individuals. One should not lightly dismiss violations of traditional American liberties merely because they affect directly only a small group of people in an isolated state. The liberties of one are the liberties of all; and what one state can do by way of "experiment," all states may adopt as standard practice. These are especially important questions during times of national (or local) stress, for then all the weaknesses of the state political systems are likely to combine to produce hasty, ill-considered,

and extreme measures, which once adopted outlive the situation which gave them their initial justification. . . .

The argument for judicial self-restraint where states and civil liberties are concerned, however, is most often stated in the terms used by Frankfurter . . . : one should depend on the self-corrective possibilities of the democratic process. Clearly, however, such self-purging is likely only when there actually is a meaningful democratic process. The points I have raised here indicate—to put it mildly—that one may have doubts on this score. Neither the process nor the result is democratic. If it is not, then the self-correction argument is invalid and it becomes at least an open question whether the courts should intervene to protect either process or result.

At this point the critic will perhaps interject: "But to say that there is a *need* for protection hardly proves that the courts can or should provide it." Granted. But given the existence in our Constitution of the Bill of Rights, it can at least provide the data on which a theory of the judicial function can be built. Such a theory was developed by Justice Stone in his well-known "doctrine of political restraints," although it is doubtful that Stone was thoroughly conversant with all the facts presented above. His idea is no more, in substance, than the feeling that where one cannot depend on the states' political institutions to correct abuses of individual rights, the federal courts are constitutionally justified in abrogating state action through judicial review. . . .

The possession of a general police power by the states is also a factor to be considered, since it gives them greater potential control over civil liberties than is possessed by the federal government. Justice Jackson pointed this out, dissenting in the Beauharnais case, when he said, "the evils at which Congress may aim, and in so doing come into conflict with free speech, will be relatively few since it is a government of limited powers. Because the states may reach more evils, they will have wider range to punish speech. . . ." He might have added, though he did not, that this very fact justifies a "more exacting judicial scrutiny" of state civil liberties cases than of some other kinds of litigation.

It should perhaps be emphasized that the concern here is not so much with democracy *per se*, but rather with constitutional democracy—that is, with that protection of minority groups and individuals which is necessary to a democracy. Thus, I am not trying to say that the Supreme Court is more democratic than any particular state government: one can hardly measure the degree of democracy so precisely. Nor would I wish to espouse a position which would

justify judicial review for cases from Georgia but not for those from Wisconsin—although *in substance* criminal cases from Illinois and race cases from any southern state indicate that something of this sort does happen. Judicial review is needed wherever minority rights are violated. They are violated at some time in any state, for reasons which have been indicated in this analysis. Sometimes such violations are, no doubt, due to excesses of democracy, but perhaps more often to its malfunctioning. In either case the important thing is the violation, not the reason for it. . . .

CONSTITUTIONALISM AND THE STATES

From a constitutional point of view there seems no reason why the states should not be treated in the same manner as the federal government. Although it is true that ours is a federal system, so that the states have "rights," it is true also that these rights (as well as limitations) flow from the national Constitution: this was settled by the

Civil War and the Reconstruction Amendments. States, no more than the federal government, should not be allowed to violate constitutional commands. The major problem of constitutional interpretation has seldom been "What is the status of the states?" but rather, "What does the Constitution command?". . .

J. Skelly Wright

THE ROLE OF THE SUPREME COURT IN A DEMOCRATIC SOCIETY — JUDICIAL ACTIVISM OR RESTRAINT?

Judge J. Skelly Wright sits on the United States Court of Appeals for the District of Columbia. He has long been an active champion of judicial involvement in social and political issues. His writings and his opinions reflect this attitude.

ONE of the Warren Court's severest critics tells us that during the Chief Justice's tenure the Supreme Court has "wrought more fundamental changes in the political and legal structure of the United States than during

any similar span of time since the Marshall Court had the unique opportunity to express itself on a [clean slate]." This has distressed those who counsel judicial restraint.

Remembering that certain past Su-

Source: *The Cornell Law Review*, Vol. 54, No. 1 (1968). Copyright © 1968 by Cornell University.

preme Courts, particularly those of the twenties and early thirties, also tried to play an active role in shaping our society, the apostles of restraint warn that even though we may approve the results that the Warren Court has decreed, we still must chastise the Court for assuming an activist role. For even if the changes are desirable, they say the Court is not the proper institution to initiate them. Rather, the sorts of judgments the Court has made are the province of the legislatures; and, of course, the Court must not legislate. After all, it was the illicit role of a super legislature that the Nine Old Men are said to have assumed.

These critics are particularly upset because, just as many of the ill-fated "activist" decisions of the past were decided by recourse to the open-ended concept of substantive due process, so many of the Warren Court's path-breaking decisions have been rendered pursuant to the equally open-ended concepts of equal protection and procedural due process. It is into these generalized constitutional commands that the Justices are most likely to read their own personal predilections and thus render ad hoc justice. Consequently, both the old Court and the Warren Court are criticized for much the same reasons.

There is, however, an obvious difference between the two Courts. The Nine Old Men were trying to halt a revolution in the role of government as a social instrument, while the Warren Court is obviously furthering that effort. Its most significant pronouncements have decreed change in the status quo, not its preservation. Rather than invalidate legislative efforts at social progress, its decisions have ordered alteration of widespread and long accepted practices, including many which had not been legislatively sanctioned in the first place. In Professor Berle's phrase, the Warren Court has functioned as a "revolutionary committee."

Simply to say, however, that the Warren Court has frequently ordered change while the old Court tried to halt it does not itself establish that the one has done a good job and the other a bad one. Nor does it establish that either Court should have acted at all. It is my contention that the Warren Court has not simply decreed the right results, but also that it was right to have decreed them. Its active role in shaping our society has been a necessary and proper one. It is, then, necessary to distinguish its performance from that of certain "activist" Courts of the past whose performances were certainly injudicious. . . .

JUDICIAL REVIEW IN A DEMOCRACY

Despite what has . . . been said, there can of course be no doubt that ours is essentially a society where the exercise of power draws its legitimacy from the consent of the people. Moreover, the sort of society we are going to have is to be determined by the people. Our faith is not simply in our ability to choose wise rulers, but in our ability to rule ourselves wisely. Learned Hand was not alone when he said that he would find it irksome to be ruled by a bevy of platonic guardians even if he knew how to choose them.

The Court, then, is not to function as a nine-man bevy, reviewing legislation from the same, but presumably more enlightened, perspective as the legisla-

ture. When the majority, speaking through the legislature, has decided that the legislation is desirable, it is not for the Court to strike it down simply because it thinks otherwise. Yet whenever the Court strikes down legislation, it says to the majority that it may not have its own way. If the Court is to refrain from doing this simply because the Justices find the status quo preferable, when and on what basis is it to strike down legislation? What are the Court's institutional characteristics that enable it to bring to the appraisal of legislation a new and different perspective unavailable to the legislature? How can the Court presume to say to the present majority that it cannot have its own way because its wishes are contrary to its own fundamental principles?

But just as an individual may be untrue to himself, so may society be untrue to itself. The Court's reviewing function, then, can be seen as an attempt to keep the community true to its own fundamental principles. Maintaining these "enduring general values" of the community is a task for which the Court's structure makes it peculiarly well suited. Professor Bickel suggests that judges have, or should have, the leisure, the training, and the insulation to follow the ways of the scholar in pursuing the ends of government. This is crucial to sorting out the enduring values of a society. And it is not something that institutions can do well on occasion, while operating for the most part with a different set of gears.

Moreover, in considering questions of principle, courts are presented with the reality of their application. Statutes deal typically with abstract or sometimes dimly foreseen problems. Courts are concerned with the flesh and blood of an actual case. This tends to modify, perhaps to lengthen, everyone's view. It also provides an extremely salutary proving ground for all abstractions; it is conducive, in a phrase of Holmes, to thinking things, not words, and thus to the evolution of principle by a process that tests as it creates. "Their insulation and the marvelous mystery of time give courts the capacity to appeal to men's better natures, to call forth their aspirations, which may have been forgotten in the moment's hue and cry." This is what Justice Stone called the opportunity for "the sober second thought." Charles Black put it more concisely when he termed judicial review "the people's institutionalized means of self-control."

This conception of judicial review, casting the Court as the guardian of enduring principle and as a check on overzealous legislatures, depicts the Court as an essentially conservative rather than creative force in our society —hardly the "revolutionary committee" Professor Berle has called the Warren Court. The political and social realities of the twentieth century, however, have required government to essay an affirmative role in its service to its citizens. The Court, as part of government, must participate in that affirmative role.

This, of course, does not minimize the importance of protecting fundamental individual rights from governmental invasion. The original Bill of Rights was essentially negative, putting beyond the reach of government the world of the spirit and raising procedural barriers to governmental intrusion. The definition of these barriers in opinions such as Brandeis's dissent in *Olmstead* or his concurrence in *Whitney,* which have since carried the day, has been crucially important in charting the direction in which our society has moved. But today, as Archibald Cox put it:

[T]he political theory which acknowledges the duty of government to provide jobs, social security, medical care, and housing extends to the field of human rights and imposes an obligation to promote liberty, equality, and dignity. For a decade and a half recognition of this duty [of the Court] has been the most creative force in constitutional law.

The more traditional rationales of judicial review do not quite fit when the Court's role is so utterly different. Yet the specter of the Court ruling the people persists and is, if anything, even more ominous where the Court is telling the government what it must do, not simply what it cannot do. What, then, is the Court's legitimate role in delineating constitutional duties? Again, the legitimacy of the Court's decrees must be derived from the community itself. Just as society may not be true to its enduring principles, so may it not be fully aware of its emerging ones. And just as the Court should maintain the one set of principles, so should it support and encourage the adoption of others.

The law need not, as Learned Hand suggested, "be content to lag behind the best inspiration of its time until it feels behind it the weight of such general acceptance as will give sanction to its pretension to unquestioned dictation." Rather, the Court must foster the best inspiration of the time and help it win general acceptance.

Nevertheless, inspiration is "best," not simply because the individual Justices think so, but because it accords with the ideals of the community itself. Today the most important of those ideals is political equality, and the Warren Court is correct in perceiving it as the dominant theme of American political development. The accuracy of this perception gives the Court's equal protection pronouncements their legitimacy.

It was the inaccuracy of the old Court's perception of community ideals that made its performance so bad. For what the Nine Old Men tried to put beyond the reach of government, both state and federal, was "the momentous issue of the welfare state itself"—an issue so political that it cannot and should not be determined by a court. It is certainly not an issue about which there is a consensus in the community, moral or otherwise. It is in fact *the* issue around which politics in this country has generally been divided. "Principles" bearing on the issue, though fervently believed by those professing them, are utterly conflicting. Unlike the ideal of political equality, they represent the creeds of particular political parties, but are not the enduring principles of our society itself. The issue of the welfare state must, and will, be "determined by 'dominant opinion' with or without judicial approval." Yet this was just the issue which the old Court told the people they could not determine for themselves by trying to place the minimum wage, the federal income tax, and government price control beyond the majority's reach.

To some critics, the Warren Court's implementation of political equality has also seemed a novel and illegitimate judicial theme. Equality, however, is not a novel ideal at all. It is only that the range of its required application is becoming broader and more evident as the community becomes aware of the extent to which the world of the poor and of the Negro differs from that in which the bulk of the public lives. The apparent novelty of the Court's recent equal protection decisions stems "from the Court's partial recognition, reflecting a new awareness on the part of the public, that the freedom embodied in constitutional guarantees as they have historically been limited is, for the economically and socially disadvantaged, no freedom at all."

In this context, and in the era of positive government, it is incumbent on the Court to protect unpopular minorities not simply from governmental persecution, but from governmental neglect as well. For just as there are certain groups in society that have proved politically advantageous to oppress, so there are others whose interests are consistently bypassed by the political process in the rush toward the great society. This explains the necessity for affirmative decrees.

Because the Warren Court, unlike the old Court, has affirmatively applied the true principles and ideals of our community to protect those whose interests go unprotected elsewhere, it has acted properly. . . .

"Once loosed, the idea of Equality is not easily cabined." Nevertheless, the Court's equal protection decisions have avoided the twin dangers posed by the judicial implementation of the egalitarian ideal. First, the Court has recognized that our egalitarianism is not, and is not likely to become, one of maximum *material* equality among people. We still believe in material rewards for individual accomplishment. It is only, therefore, in certain limited areas that equality between rich and poor is a moral principle of our society. Where such equality is a part of our ideals, however, the Court is right to decree its realization even if the political branches have been unwilling to pay for its implementation. The Court was correct in singling out the criminal process and the franchise for such treatment, since in these areas the relationship of the individual to his government should not depend on the ability to pay.

A second danger which the Court must continue to avoid is the choking of the political process with the equal protection clause. For almost all legislation is advantageous to some groups and disadvantageous to others, and often in a somewhat arbitrary way. Nevertheless, this sort of give and take within the political process, particularly where economic regulation is challenged, should not become the concern of the Court. Unlike the old Court, the current Court has specifically eschewed responsibility in this area.

Railway Express Agency v. New York is illustrative. Railway Express challenged a New York City traffic ordinance forbidding advertising on the sides of trucks, the theory being that it distracted drivers of other vehicles. Those trucks whose advertisements were connected with the owner's business, however, were exempted from the ordinance. Railway Express, which sold advertising space on its delivery trucks, argued that simply because one is touting one's own product does not make his sign any the less a distraction to other drivers. Railway Express of course was right. The statute *did* draw an arbitrary, unreasonable distinction. Mr. Justice Douglas, however, was also right in rejecting the argument, saying, "It is no requirement of equal protection that all evils of the same genus be eradicated or none at all." One can confidently surmise that in the New York City council the small business interests were sufficiently powerful to block the regulation altogether unless they were granted exemption from it. Granted, they won special "irrational" dispensation. But surely the legislation did not discriminate *against* Railway Express. Interpreted otherwise, equal protection could become as debilitating to welfare legislation as the ill-fated doctrine of substantive due process once was.

The Court must continue carefully to distinguish those groups whose rights are consistently trammelled and whose interests are consistently neglected in the political arena, from those groups whose interests are occasionally submerged in legislative compromise. This the Court has done. It has applied and extended the principles and ideals of our society to those "insular" minorities which, either because they are unpopular or because the vindication of their rights is expensive, are persecuted or neglected by the legislatures. In so doing, it has tried to secure the integrity of the legislative processes themselves. These are tasks for which the courts, the "deviant" institutions in our democratic society, are required.

In three 1966 cases interpreting Congress's powers to enforce equal protection pursuant to section 5 of the fourteenth amendment, the Supreme Court has given Congress almost free rein where the Fuller Court had curtailed it in the *Civil Rights Cases*. As Professor Cox has said, "If the Congress follows the lead that the Court has provided, [these cases] . . . will prove as important in bespeaking national legislative authority to promote human rights as the Labor Board decisions of 1937 were in providing national authority to regulate the economy." Congressional action, however, is a big "if." For as Cox also warns, "the need for judicial action is strongest in the areas of the law where political processes prove inadequate, not from lack of legislative power but because the problem is neglected by politicians." If the legislatures continue to neglect their constitutional responsibilities, we can only hope the Court will continue to do the best it can to fill the gap.

VI. FACING THE REALITY OF A POLITICAL COURT: A CRITICAL ANALYSIS

Philip B. Kurland

TOWARD A POLITICAL SUPREME COURT

Philip B. Kurland, professor of law at the University of Chicago, has been gaining increasing recognition during the past few years as a highly qualified observer of the Supreme Court. Sensitive to any institution accruing inordinate power, including the Presidency, Professor Kurland in this selection looks at the practical effects of a political Supreme Court in the American governmental system.

OBVIOUSLY the Supreme Court is more than the nine individuals gowned in black and ensconced in the marble palace in Washington. Like the Presidency and the Congress, the Court must be viewed as an institution separate and apart from those who temporarily occupy the offices. It is important to examine the Court's actions and to evaluate its use of power not just for today. Like Maitland, one must take a deep account of yesterday in order that today not paralyze tomorrow.

The ardent advocates of enhancement of presidential power when John F. Kennedy occupied the White House seem to have lost most of their ardor during the more recent tenures of Presidents Johnson and Nixon. Those prepared to have the congressional role in foreign affairs and the Senate's power to review treaty commitments bypassed for more efficient methods have begun to recognize the values inherent in such checks on the executive will, as the Viet Nam tragedy becomes ever more tragic. And, now, with a radical change of personnel on the Supreme Court already begun, there must be at least some advocates of judicial power prepared to think in more institutional terms.

For, just as the power flowing to the national government from the states became irreversible at some point in our history; just as the accretion of executive authority and the reduction of legislative authority has become intractable; so, too, the authority that the Court might assert—and the manner of its assertion—could become fixed for use by Justices who succeed those who first utilize it. I do not mean that these trends cannot be reversed. Certainly they can, but only at the cost of weathering a constitutional crisis with all its correlative consequences and dangers.

The proper question about the Court today—before the crisis is upon us—is not whether we should reverse the flow of authority, but whether it should be slowed or speeded. The question is whether the essential function that only the Court performs will be strengthened or weakened by further quick movements of the Supreme Court along the road that it has recently travelled.

We have it on very high authority that the Supreme Court's functions should be expanded and legitimized. Professor Berle tells us that withdrawal

Source: *The University of Chicago Law Review*, Vol. 37 (1969), pp. 19–45.

from power, apparently like withdrawal from drugs, would have most unpleasant consequences.

A corollary to the first law of power (that it always replaces chaos) is an implacable rule. Power cast aside without provision for its further exercise almost invariably destroys the abdicating power holder—as, for example, Shakespeare's King Lear found out when he improvidently abandoned his power, and was promptly crushed. Conceivably, the Supreme Court might have avoided assuming the power position in the first place—but it cannot renounce it now. It has entered, created, and accepted a field of responsibility. Elements in that field might wreck the Court were it now to desert the function it has assumed.

I do not know whether Lear's kingdom would have been better off had he remained in authority. Nor do I know that the Congress and the President are properly analogized to Goneril, Regan, and Cordelia or their husbands. After all, we have seen that the administration of the realm of civil rights, so far from perfect as it is, had become more effective as Congress and the executive took over control than when it was the sole concern of the judiciary. In any event, the proper question is not abdication, but how the Court's authority should be exercised.

I suggest that we ask whether, as the Warren Court has moved toward the legislative mode and away from the judicial mode of carrying on its business, it has endangered the capacity to perform its peculiar function. A truly legislative body, as the Court itself has frequently said, must be directly responsible to the expression of majority will. The single institution in our system created for the purpose of protecting the interests of minorities—assuming that is what the Constitution is about, at least in part—is the Supreme Court. Its essentially anti-democratic character keeps it constantly in jeopardy of destruction. But that characteristic is both its principal virtue and its primary limitation. The question is do we secure more of what we need or want by turning the Supreme Court into a third legis-

lative chamber, or by retaining it in the form of a judicial body.

It should be clear, even to the blindest partisan, that the Court has never been either purely judicial or purely legislative in its work. I should like, however, to examine some of its processes to suggest that it has in recent years been moving toward the legislative pole. I reject the notion that this is determinable simply by examining its conclusions and deciding whether the Court has made new law. If the Supreme Court did not make new law, it would be hard to justify its existence. Fixed principles are as readily applied by lower federal courts and by state courts as by the nine berobed men in Washington. The issue is rather how that new law is made and why, and what effect it will or should have.

Some political scientists and some self-styled realists among the lawyers would say that the Court is in fact already a legislative body, or is not different from a legislative body in its function. Indeed, Professor Berle's recent tantalizing little book opens with the proposition that "Ultimate legislative power in the United States has come to rest in the Supreme Court of the United States." But this position, it seems to me, rests on an oversimplified notion of how the legislative function differs from the judicial. I submit that the difference does not lie in whether one or the other has a lawmaking power. There may be some—even in this day—who are unwilling to recognize that courts make law. But our legal heritage derives from the great tradition of the common law which originated at a time when the courts were the prime lawmakers and the legislature was new to the function. And I am assured by Professor Kalven that, as he surveys developments in the field of tort law, he is convinced that the common-law courts are as creative today as they ever were. At least since Holmes' day, we have recognized judicial lawmaking as a conscious process of creation, not discovery. . . .

The distinction that I am seeking to draw here between the juridical mode and the legislative mode is a distinction between two rule-making processes. When I suggest that the Warren Court has moved closer to the legislative form than most of its predecessors have done, it is not because it has made new law, but because in making new law it has come closer to emulating the legislative process than any of its predecessors. But I should emphasize that the Court still has a long way to go before identity of the processes will have occurred. For, I would repeat, one essential difference between the two systems lies in their respective constituencies. The legislature represents that combination of groups and individuals that makes a majority on any issue; the Court's primary obligations are to discrete minorities. The majority is an ever-present threat to the Court's authority, and must be taken into account for that reason. And no one suggests openly that where the majority will is expressed through legislation, it is the Court's function to thwart it or prevent it. The exception is where the legislature imposes on individuals or minorities in so fundamental a fashion as to necessitate invoking the safeguards of the Constitution.

Comparing the role of the common-law judge to that of the legislator, Cardozo, in the Holmes tradition, said:

My analysis of the judicial process comes then to this, and little more: logic and history, and custom, and utility, and the accepted standards of right conduct, are the forces which singly or in combination shape the progress of the law. Which of these forces shall dominate in any case, must depend largely upon the comparative importance or value of the social interests that will be thereby promoted or impaired. One of the most fundamental social interests is that law shall be uniform and impartial. There must be nothing in its action that savors of prejudice or favor or even arbitrary whim or fitfulness. Therefore in the main there shall be adherence to precedent . . . .

If you ask how he [the judge] is to know when one interest outweighs another, I can only answer that he must get his knowledge just as the legislator gets it, from experience and study and reflection; in brief, from life itself. Here, indeed, is the point of contact between the legislator's

work and his. The choice of methods, the appraisement of values, must in the end be guided by like considerations for the one as for the other. Each indeed is legislating within the limits of his competence. No doubt the limits for the judge are narrower. He legislates only between gaps. He fills the open spaces in the law. How far he may go without traveling beyond the walls of the interstices cannot be staked out for him upon a chart. He must learn it for himself as he gains the sense of fitness and proportion that comes with years of habitude in the practice of an art. Even within the gaps, restrictions not easy to define, but felt, however impalpable they may be, by every judge and lawyer, hedge and circumscribe his action. They are established by the traditions of the centuries, by the example of other judges, his predecessors and his colleagues, by the collective judgment of the profession, and by the duty of adherence to the pervading spirit of the law.

It is important to recognize that both Holmes and Cardozo were talking essentially about common-law courts where the analogy to legislation is closer and easier. For one thing, if the common-law courts legislate interstitially, they also legislate only temporarily. If the legislature chooses a different rule from that pronounced by the courts, in the common-law world the legislative will is dominant. This is the point made by J. R. Lucas in differentiating the English high court from the Supreme Court:

The example of the Supreme Court of the United States of America shows that if we want to keep politics out of the administration of justice, we must deprive the officials who administer justice of all discretion which might be influenced by political considerations. Else there will be an incentive for politicians to attempt to "pack" the courts with their own partisans. But where the ultimate authority is a non-judicial court or assembly, all we need to ensure when selecting people to be judges is that they shall faithfully apply the laws enacted by the Legislature in all cases to which they clearly apply. It was not necessary to pack the English Bench because the same judges who decided the Taff Vale case could be relied upon, whatever their political opinions or private views, to apply the provisions of the Trades Disputes Act, which reversed the Taff Vale decision. Provided the judges, like reeds, will bow to political winds in due legislative form, there is no reason for them not to exercise, in the absence of a clear directive from Parliament, their own judgment on what is equitable and just. All that we do demand is that where Parliament has given a ruling, judges should follow it, even against their own judgment, not because Parliament is wiser, more equitable or more just than the judges, but . . . because it is expedient to concentrate all political discretion in Parliament, where, though wrong may be done, it will be done openly.

. . . This supremacy of the legislature is missing in constitutional litigation. And thus there is an additional important distinction between common-law judicial legislation and that kind indulged by the Supreme Court of the United States. Common-law issues, by definition, are problems submitted for resolution by the judiciary in the absence of statutory attempts at resolving them. Constitutional adjudication, on the other hand, never takes place at so early a stage in the search for a solution to the social, political, or economic problem presented. It is not until one of the other branches of government has faced the problem and exercised or refused to exercise its law-making powers that the judiciary is called on to decide a constitutional issue. It is this factor of prior rule making by legislative or executive decision that inheres in constitutional cases and is absent from the list of intangibles described by Holmes and Cardozo in their description of judicial legislation.

Indeed, it is this factor that has really brought forth the charge that the Warren Court has improperly become a legislature. That charge is, in effect, that the Court did not give adequate weight to the conclusions reached by other branches of government, at least equally appropriate bodies for ascertaining proper public policy. And Professor Berle's claim that the Court has become a super-legislature is a claim to the power to discount the judgment of other governmental authorities in deciding what rule is best. In essence, the attack is that the Court has failed to subscribe to the Thayer thesis about judicial review. Thayer put it this way in his biography of John Marshall:

To set aside the acts of such a body [a legislature], representing in its own field, which is the very highest of all, the ultimate sovereign, should be a solemn, unusual, and painful act. Something is wrong when it can ever be other than that. And if it be true that the holders of legislative power are careless or evil, yet the constitutional duty of the court remains untouched; it cannot rightly attempt to protect the people, by undertaking a function not its own. On the other hand, by adhering rigidly to its own duty, the court will help, as nothing else can, to fix the spot where the responsibility lies, and to bring down on the precise locality the thunderbolt of popular condemnation. The judiciary, today, in dealing with the acts of their coordinate legislators, owe to the country no greater or clearer duty than that of keeping their hands off these acts wherever it is possible to do it. For that course—the true course of judicial duty always—will powerfully help to bring the people and their representatives to a sense of their responsibility. There will still remain to the judiciary an ample field for the determination of their remarkable jurisdiction, of which our American law has so much reason to be proud; a jurisdiction which has some of its chief illustrations and its greatest triumphs, as in Marshall's time, so in ours, while the courts were refusing to exercise it.

Certainly if the small number of cases of invalidation of national legislation are to be taken as the test, the validity of the charge that the Court has improperly legislated in the area of constitutional review is debatable. . . .

There are other complaints about the Court's judicial legislation at the constitutional level. One is Mr. Justice Black's that the Court frequently does not justify its legislation by any command of the Constitution. In essence this is a rejection not only of constitutional judicial legislation but equally of that kind described by Holmes and Cardozo. During the last part of the last Term of the Warren Court, Mr. Justice Black, in dissent, expressed his attitude in this manner:

The latest statement by my Brother HARLAN on the power of this Court under the Due Process Clause to hold laws unconstitutional on the ground of the Justices' view of "fundamental fairness" makes it necessary for me to add a few words in order that the difference between us be made absolutely clear. He now says that the Court's idea of "fundamental fairness" is derived "not alone . . . from the specifics of the Constitution, but also . . . from concepts which are part of the Anglo-American legal heritage." This view is consistent with that expressed by Mr. Justice Frankfurter in *Rochin v. California* that due process was to be determined by "those canons of decency and fairness which express the notions of justice of English-speaking peoples. . . ." 342 U.S. 168. In any event my Brother HARLAN's "Anglo-American legal heritage" is no more definite than the "notions of justice of the English-speaking peoples" or the shock-the-conscience test. All these so-called tests represent nothing more or less than an implicit adoption of a Natural Law concept which under our system leaves to judges alone the power to decide what the Natural Law means. These so-called standards do not bind judges within any boundaries that can be precisely marked or defined by words for holding laws unconstitutional. On the contrary, these tests leave them wholly free to decide what they are convinced is right and fair. If the judges, in deciding whether laws are constitutional, are to be left only to the admonitions of their own consciences, why was it that the Founders gave us a written Constitution at all?

The Justice asks what is certainly a basic and difficult question. And he states as well as anyone another meaning of the charge of judicial legislation. One cannot really answer his question, except by rejecting the alternative that he suggests. Is it worse for the Court to read commands inhibitory of government from amorphous phrases that were put there by the Constitution's authors than to read the same commands into specific language that can accommodate them only with even more difficulty? What is the meaning to be given to such loose phrases as due process of law in the fifth amendment, or republican form of government in the fourth article, or privileges and immunities as used in the fourth article, or equal protection of the laws as in the fourteenth amendment? How can a strict constructionist, so-

called, like Black have acquiesced in the reapportionment cases? The answer to Black and others voicing this same criticism can be found in the description of judicial legislation in the quotations above from Cardozo and Holmes. Frankfurter, against whom Black leveled this attack again and again, has said:

It may be that responsibility for decisions dulls the capacity for discernment. The fact is that one sometimes envies the certitude of outsiders [as well as some Justices?] regarding the compulsions to be drawn from vague and admonitory constitutional provisions. Only for those who have not the responsibility of decision can it be easy to decide the grave and complex problems they raise, especially in controversies that excite public interest. This is so because they too often present legal issues inextricably and deeply bound up in emotional reactions to sharply conflicting economic, social, and political views. It is not the duty of judges to express their personal attitudes on such issues, deep as their individual convictions may be. The opposite is the truth; it is their duty not to act on merely personal views. But "due process," once we go beyond its strictly procedural aspect, and the "equal protection of the laws" enshrined in the Constitution, are precisely defined neither by history nor in terms. . . .
No doubt, these provisions of the Constitution were not calculated to give permanent legal sanction merely to the social arrangements and beliefs of a particular epoch. Like all legal provisions without a fixed technical meaning, they are ambulant, adaptable to changes of time. That is their strength; that also makes dubious their appropriateness for judicial enforcement. Dubious because their vagueness readily lends itself to make of the Court a third chamber with drastic veto power. This danger has been pointed out by our greatest judges too often to be dismissed as a bogey. Holding democracy in judicial tutelage is not the most promising way to foster disciplined responsibility in a people.

On the other hand, it might be said that "holding democracy in judicial tutelage" is the only way that has yet been devised for preventing the "tyranny of the majority," as Mill termed it, from imposing on the minority. This aspect of what Frankfurter's good friend Lord Radcliffe termed "The Problem of Power" remains the central problem of

American life, not merely in terms of judicial problems but also because of those created by the executive and the legislature in their exclusive spheres of authority.

Yet, it must be conceded to Mr. Justice Black and others that, to the extent that the Court's discretion has become less and less fettered by the judgments of its coordinate branches of the national government, by the decisions of various state agencies, by the language of the Constitution and federal statutes, it is behaving more and more like a legislative body and less and less like a court.

To the extent, too, that the Court's lawmaking is not justified by well-reasoned opinions, it is indulging a privilege that belongs more to a legislature than to an appellate court. The Supreme Court's own rules impose on federal trial courts an obligation to justify their judgments by stated findings of fact and conclusions of law. That rule has two functions. One is to make the trial court more aware of the problems that it is confronting. The other is to justify its results to a reviewing tribunal. But as Mr. Justice Jackson was fond of reminding his brethren, the reason that the Supreme Court does not have to meet this same obligation of justifying its results is only that there is no other court which can hold it responsible. "We are not final because we are infallible, . . . we are infallible only because we are final."

Strangely, the defenders of the Warren Court do not tend to argue that its opinions are well reasoned, but rather that they are no worse than John Marshall's classic judgments. The defect was put in these terms by Professors Bickel and Wellington of the Yale Law School:

The Court's product has shown an increasing incidence of the sweeping dogmatic statement, of the formulation of results accompanied by little or no effort to support them in reason, in sum, of opinions that do not opine and of per curiam orders that quite frankly fail to build the bridge between the authorities they cite and the results they decree.

The defense is not that the Court should not do better, but that it has sometimes been as bad in the past as in the present. Again, we are on the border of legislative prerogative to create rules without the need for justifying them.

Worse, however, is that this kind of opinion writing has led to the evils that disturbed Mr. Justice Cardozo when he was faced with the same kind of behavior by the majority of the Nine Old Men with whom he sat. The problem of which Cardozo wrote is endemic in American society, but one looks to the Court for higher standards than those of the hustings or of Madison Avenue. In *Snyder v. Massachusetts*, Cardozo wrote:

A fertile source of perversion in constitutional theory is the tyranny of labels. Out of the vague precepts of the Fourteenth Amendment a court frames a rule which is general in form, though it has been wrought under the pressure of particular situations. Forthwith another situation is placed under the rule because it is fitted to the words, though related faintly, if at all, to the reasons that brought the rule into existence.

Certainly the decisions that followed hard on the heels of *Brown v. Board of Education* fit the description that is contained in the quotation from Cardozo. And this derives, I would suggest, from the notion that the judgment of the Court is not a resolution of a case or controversy, but rather is an edict no different in form or consequence than a statute.

The old theory was that a court resolves a particular case that has been submitted to it. Its judgment is binding on all who were parties to the litigation. Indeed, it is said to be unconstitutional to bind those who were not parties to the litigation. In form, the Court's judgments do not purport to control the behavior of any except those who were brought under its jurisdiction. At the same time, the opinions form an ample basis for prediction so that they meet Holmes' test, at least, of the meaning of law: "The prophecies of what the courts will do in fact, and nothing more pretentious, are what I mean by law."

Legislation, on the other hand, is premised on the proposition that it is

directed to the entire population within
the domain, or such portion of it as falls
within the ken of the statute. Even if
the executive or judicial power may be
necessary to enforce it, the obligation is
created by the statute. The distinction
I have in mind may be revealed by
pointing out the differences between the
desegregation judgment in *Brown* and
its coverage and the obligations created
by the Civil Rights Acts of more recent
vintage. The former, however clear its
implications for those subjected to further litigation, created no duties except
on those parties to the law suit. The
statutes imposed duties on all within
their ambits. . . . Congress is, of course,
not bound to adhere to decisions that it
has made at earlier times. It can reverse itself as often as a majority thinks
it appropriate to do so, without being
called to account for its inconsistency.
So, too, apparently with the Warren
Court. It has paid less heed to stare
decisis—one of the features that Cardozo pointed out as distinguishing legislative legislation from judicial legislation—than any Supreme Court in
history. It started by overruling *Plessy v.
Ferguson* and ended by destroying *Palko
v. Connecticut*. In between a very large
number of constitutional landmarks
that once were "the law of the land"
were made into artifacts for the study
of historians. Nor did it make a difference that some cases that were overruled were venerable while others were
creatures of the Warren Court itself.

If some of these features of the legislative process to which the Warren
Court adhered had also been indulged,
if to a lesser degree, by earlier Courts,
the next analogy to which I would call
your attention was totally novel to the
Warren Court. The United States reports are full of statements suggesting
a distinction between legislation and judicial lawmaking in terms of the prospective or retrospective application of
the resultant rules. For examples: Mr.
Justice Brewer once said: "One often-
declared difference between judicial and
legislative power is that . . . the one construes what has been; the other determines what shall be." Mr. Justice Pitney

asserted that: "Legislation consists in
laying down laws or rules for the future." And Mr. Justice McKenna wrote:
"Statutes are addressed to the future, not
the past." The theme is constantly reiterated. They did not say that legislation could never be retroactive. "There
is no constitutional inhibition against
retrospective laws. Though generally
distrusted, they are often beneficial, and
sometimes necessary." But nowhere was
there any hint that judicial decisions
could be solely prospective in their
nature.

It was the Warren Court that initiated
the practice of imitating the legislature
by providing that its decisions in certain
criminal cases, where it avowedly
changed the meaning of the Constitution from what it had been, would have
only prospective effect. . . .

There are still other ways in which
the legislative process was imitated by
the Warren Court. One of them relates
to the practice of amicus curiae briefs.
Frederick Bernays Wiener, the reporter
for the Supreme Court's committee on
the revision of its rules that were
effected in 1954 has written on the subject in a way that reveals the issue:

That the presentation of briefs *amicus
curiae* had become a problem was evidenced
by the 1949 amendment to old Rule 27(9).
In fact, such briefs were no longer presented only by parties with cases or interests similar to or identical with those actually before the Court; they had become a
vehicle for propaganda efforts. Far from
affording assistance to the Justices, on
occasion they did not even mention the
decisive issue on which the case turned and
which divided the Court. Instead their emphasis was on the size and importance of
the group represented, or on contempora-
neous press comment adverse to the ruling
of the Court. Certainly there were multiplying signs after 1947 that the brief
amicus curiae had become essentially an
instrumentality designed to exert extrajudicial pressure on judicial decisions . . . .

The stringent rule adopted in 1949 was
continued by the 1954 rules.

Despite the supposed stringency of
the rule, however, and in no small part
due to pressure by Mr. Justice Frank-

furter, the practice was relaxed. The Warren Court has been inundated with exactly the kind of amicus curiae briefs described by Wiener. What we have come to see is the development of a lobbying practice, more decorous than the ones used in the legislative halls, but directed to the same ends. The Court instead of squelching the practice has encouraged it.

There is still another aspect of the amicus brief that is a reminder of the legislative process. I have suggested elsewhere that no major congressional legislation has been forthcoming except at the request or direction of the President. It is not that the legislation necessarily takes the form that the President desires. It is rather that the executive's views must be taken into account before the legislative decision is reached. The same is becoming true in the Supreme Court. The views of the Solicitor General's Office have been offered or requested in almost all the major litigation that has come before the Court in recent years and in a good deal of litigation that cannot qualify as important. The effect of the Solicitor General's amicus briefs, for example, is well known with regard to such cases as *Brown* and *Baker v. Carr.* Whether the executive branch of government, which is also the chief litigant before the Court, ought to act in such an advisory capacity in cases in which it has no direct interest is a question that has not been raised. I do not offer an answer here. Again, I emphasize only the trend toward the legislative process that has come about in the conduct of the Warren Court's business.

Two more such analogies and I am done with them. Neither may seem important. Both display imitation of congressional behavior by Justices of the high court. The first is the multiplying occasions on which the Justices have taken to the hustings in defense of their opinions or in anticipation of those that they have not yet written. Supreme Court Justices have always been in demand as speakers for bar associations and law schools. But they used to restrain themselves both in the number of occasions on which they would speak and in the subject matter that they were willing to address. This is all changed. . . . What we have received, . . . is not merely restatement of the Court's decisions, but commitments to positions made in advance of argument and hearing on cases that were to come before the Court. . . .

My final parallel between the Court and the legislative process relates to the crisis that develops at the end of each of their respective terms. Both the Court and Congress have the tendency to put off decision of their most important problems until adjournment is in the offing. Then we have what has appropriately been called "decision by deadline." One has but to glance through the reports of the Warren Court to discover that the month of June in each year is the time when vast constitutional revisions are most likely to take place. Whether this is conducive to the kind of opinions that such important problems deserve is a question that should arouse great concern. Congress has some reasons for decisions close to adjournment. Congress is not a continuing body and adjournment is necessary for Congressmen to return to their electorate for the determination of whether they shall be returned to office. Then, too, budgets are annual matters with consequent pressures unmatched by those on the Court. The Court's Term, on the other hand, is a totally artificial construct. There is no necessity for adjournment in June. And there is no reason why argued cases have to be decided before the June adjournment takes place. The latter is simply a holdover from the days when Chief Justice Hughes was trying to prove that the Court could remain current with its docket against a charge by President Roosevelt that the superannuated judges were too old to perform efficiently.

Let me turn then to the problems that would be faced by a political court, some of which are already existent. First, however, let me say that I do not mean to use the adjective in any pejorative sense. A political court is one that is given or assumes the function of making national policy. Since the Court is already engaged in that task, to a degree, we must be concerned with the expansion or contraction of the Court's competence and a recognition by the Court and the public of the role it is really playing in contemporary American government. Indeed, if the Court is to become a truly political institution, its competence would also have to be recognized by the other branches of the national government as well.

The first problem with entrusting large areas of public policy to the Court for ultimate decision is that it is still, despite the changes that have been brought about, restricted to the judicial form. As an institution it still cannot act until a problem is presented to it by way of an adversary proceeding in the form of a case or controversy. This means, for one thing, that the Court cannot initiate the appropriate policy until the proper question is presented to it. I recognize that the Court has found ample excuse in some cases to speak to issues far beyond those the cases presented. And I recognize, too, that in this day of the professional litigating organizations, many questions that would never have come before the high court will now be brought to it. But the extension in these areas is still not sufficient to make the Court into a prime legislating agency.

The adversary process brings with it additional burdens. The Court's decisions have to rest on the evidence and materials brought before it by the litigants or such similar information as may be garnered by its very small staff from already existing published data. The Court, because it is a court, lacks machinery for gathering the wide range of facts and opinions that should inform the judgment of a prime policy-maker. . . .

Even Professor Berle, in his outspoken advocacy of the Court's assumption of the role of prime legislator in the national government, recognizes the difficulty:

Courts are organized and staffed and judges are trained to resolve cases and con-

troversies, and decree remedies in individual cases. But where in doing that they are expected to enunciate rules applying to multitudinous situations at the same time —that is, to legislate—the problem of collecting data and arriving at a solution certainly goes far beyond their ordinary function. It is unfair as well as unwise to expect from courts legislation reorganizing county and state governments, rearranging school districts, directing school superintendents how their schools should be administered, determining whether the education given is sufficiently uniform to constitute "equal protection of the laws."

Berle, it will be noticed, is speaking only about the problems with which the Court has already purported to deal. Obviously, there will be other problems of social policy that are even more recalcitrant than those he mentioned. He would resolve the difficulty by providing the Court with a research arm, patterned, he said, after the Council of Economic Advisers—God save the mark!— which he would call the Constitutional Council. And he would also limit the Court to the resolution of major social problems that the other branches of government failed to resolve, whether from lack of interest or lack of capacity. . . .

The Constitutional Council—certainly a body of wise men—would consist of "professors of law, men with judicial experience, men with legislative experience, and men with social awareness," to be "appointed by the President by and with the advice and consent of the Senate." I find the scheme to be of questionable feasibility. Presumably the Constitutional Council would work in the manner of a Warren Commission, a Kerner Commission, or—as is the current fashion—a presidential task force. Experience teaches me that this kind of body, like the Council of Economic Advisers, is not an efficient or effective means of discovering the facts needed for the best resolution of the problem, assuming there is a resolution of the problem. It is hard to discover a single such body that has provided a functional response to the problems presented to it.

Certainly, however, if this power is to

be added to those already exercised by the Court, some program will be necessary—Berle's or another—to provide the Court with adequate data on which to base such momentous decisions.

The second deficiency of a political court goes to the absence of a means of supervising or enforcing the decrees that it promulgates. It can issue an order, it can use marshals and lower federal courts to bring about what it has commanded. But its tools are very limited indeed. One need but recall the response of President Jackson to Marshall's judgments in the Georgia Indian cases, or Lincoln's response to the Court during the Civil War, or even Eisenhower's phlegmatic response to the *Brown* case and its subsequent events, to realize that it takes more than an ipse dixit by the Court to make its decrees realities, even for those who were before the Court, no less for the nation at large. With all appropriate acknowledgment of the intractibility of the problems with which the Court has recently dealt, neither its desegregation principles, nor its ban on school prayers, nor its revision of policy practices through the exclusionary rule can be said to have yet been enforced beyond their effect on particular litigants. It can chalk up a success in the reapportionment cases. But in the absence of public acquiescence it will need more clout than it now has to perform the more exalted function that is being wished on it. For all the talk of the famous decision in *Hobson v. Hansen,* the schools in the District of Columbia are more segregated today than they were at the time of the *Brown* decision. Hobson's choice indeed. Nor can one point to a single successful resolution of a major social or economic problem by the Court. The tragedy of *Dred Scott* remains a ghost of terrifying proportions.

Enough for me, however, to point to the problems of a political Court without naysaying those who have the wisdom and the courage to find the solutions for them.

There is a third major difficulty with what Professor Berle appropriately terms: "The Supreme Court's New Revolution." On the subject of revolutions, I concede Professor Berle's expertise, since he was a co-author of another peaceful revolution that succeeded better than many have been prepared to admit. Nonetheless, I would point out that those who would expand the authority of the Supreme Court, like other contemporary self-styled revolutionaries, assume that the power to be given to it will be readily surrendered by those who now possess it. This must be based on the claim of the moral superiority of the revolutionaries. In this case, however, the change does not even have a base of "participatory democracy" to support it. More important, perhaps, is that competition for power is seldom resolved by simple claims of moral superiority.

The power that the Supreme Court would secure would have to come from the legislative and executive branches of the national government. Insofar as it purports to come from the states, it would be taking no more than a mirage. In fact, since it is the presidency that now dominates the policy-making scene, it would have to be that branch from which the Supreme Court would have to capture its authority. It is clear, I submit, that in a contest between the President and the Court or between the Court and Congress, the Court is not likely to enhance its power, it is much more likely to see it reduced. Wise Courts, in the past, have enlarged their ken insidiously, not by direct confrontation. Every direct confrontation has found the Court engaged in a strategic retreat. And, for reasons I shall suggest shortly, the time is ripe for another *volte-face,* if the confrontation cannot be avoided. To this extent, at least, Hamilton was right when he suggested that "the least dangerous" branch has "neither FORCE nor WILL, but merely judgment" at its command. The Court's capacity to express whatever will it has is entirely dependent upon the support of public opinion. Without it, as Tocqueville told us long ago, the Justices are impotent. As of now, the Court's hold on the public is weak indeed. This would not be so if it were true, as some of us like to think it to be, that the attitudes struck in academe are representative of the best thought in society. It may be that these attitudes are the best that American society can produce—though I have my doubts. What is pellucidly clear is that they are not necessarily representative of the thinking of anyone except some of those in these sheltered groves.

Let us assume, however, that ways and means can be found for enhancing the Court's prestige and power. The question then comes, how to staff such an institution. With the Court's duties no greater than they are, the problem has proved exceedingly difficult. For example, two judges whose view of the Supreme Court's proper role cannot be called expansionist, stated the job specifications. Judge Learned Hand once said:

I venture to believe that it is as important to have a judge called upon to pass on a question of constitutional law, to have at least a bowing acquaintance with Acton and Maitland, with Thucydides, Gibbon and Carlyle, with Homer, Dante, Shakespeare and Milton, with Machiavelli, Montaigne and Rabelais, with Plato, Bacon, Hume and Kant, as with the books which have been specifically written on the subject. For in such matters everything turns upon the spirit in which he approaches the questions before him. The words he must construe are empty vessels into which he can pour nearly anything he will. Men do not gather figs of thistles, nor supply institutions from judges whose outlook is limited by parish or class. They must be aware that there are before them more than verbal problems; more than final solutions cast in generalizations of universal applicability. They must be aware of the changing social tensions in every society which make it an organism; which demand new schemata of adaptation; which will disrupt it, if rigidly confined.

That was written in 1930. And, unfortunately, Judge Learned Hand never learned by personal experience the demands made on Supreme Court Justices by their offices. In 1954, fifteen years after he ascended the high court, Mr.

Justice Frankfurter spoke to the same question:

Human society keeps changing. Needs emerge, first vaguely felt and unexpressed, imperceptibly gathering strength, steadily becoming more and more exigent, generating a force which, if left unheeded and denied response so as to satisfy the impulse behind it at least in part, may burst forth with an intensity that exacts more than reasonable satisfaction. Law as the response to those needs is not merely a system of logical deduction, though considerations of logic are far from irrelevant. Law presupposes sociological wisdom as well as logical unfolding. . . .

A judge whose preoccupation is with such matters should be compounded of the faculties that are demanded of the historian and the philosopher and the prophet. The last demand upon him—to make some forecast of the consequences of his action—is perhaps the heaviest. To pierce the curtain of the future, to give shape and visage to mysteries still in the womb of time, is the gift of imagination. It requires poetic sensibilities with which judges are rarely endowed and which their education does not normally develop. These judges, you will infer, must have something of the creative artist in them; they must have antennae registering feeling and judgment beyond logical, let alone quantitative proof.

You can readily see from these two quotations that these men, at least, thought the task of a Supreme Court Justice an awesome one. More, however, they also show that each man's notion of the ideal Supreme Court Justice is garnered from what he sees in his mirror each morning, however idealized and unrelated to the truth the image might be. The essential difficulty is that those making and confirming the Justices who take their places on the high bench—Attorneys General, Presidents, and Senators—do not see in their respective shaving glasses anything like what Hand and Frankfurter described. And it is their images that are reflected in the actual appointments. The results have been what they have been largely for this reason. It takes something of the romantic or the intellectual to appoint great Supreme Court Justices. These elements are—fortunately or unfortunately—missing from the makeups of most of those who appoint Supreme Court Justices. And so the question remains, are we willing to entrust the power that belongs to nine Platonic Guardians to men of lesser capacity? If the response is affirmative on the ground that those who exercise the power now are no better qualified, I would suggest only that they are without life tenure—just think how you would shudder today at the thought of life tenure for Presidents—and they are politically responsible directly to the people. As Learned Hand said more than once: "For myself it would be irksome to be ruled by a bevy of Platonic Guardians, even if I knew how to choose them, which assuredly I do not. If they were in charge, I should miss the stimulus of living in a society where I have, at least theoretically, some part in the direction of public affairs."

There are other difficulties in expanding the political power of the Court, including that of securing adequate time to perform its functions with "the unhurried deliberation which is essential to the formulation of sound constitutional principles."

There are few strong personal beliefs that I have about the Supreme Court. The first is that the Court is not a democratic institution, either in makeup or function. This should be seen for what it is, even at the cost of that grossest of contemporary epithets: "elitist." It is politically irresponsible and must remain so, if it would perform its primary function in today's harried society. That function, evolving at least since the days of Charles Evans Hughes, is to protect the individual against the Leviathan of government and to protect minorities against oppression by majorities.

Essentially because its most important function is anti-majoritarian, it ought not to intervene to frustrate the will of the majority except where it is essential to its functions as guardian of interests that would otherwise be unrepresented in the government of the country. It must, however, do more than tread warily. It must have the

talent and recognize the obligation to explain and perhaps persuade the majority and the majority's representatives that its reasons for frustrating majority rule are good ones.

The Warren Court accepted with a vengeance the task of protector of the individual against government and of minorities against the tyranny of majorities. But it failed abysmally to persuade the people that its judgments had been made for sound reasons. Its failure on this score was due to many causes, of which I can catalogue but a few. One is that its docket was so overcrowded with lesser business that it could not concentrate its efforts on the important constitutional questions that came before it. Second is that its communication with the public had to come through the distortions of the news media, who would not invest the time, effort, or space to the careful job that is necessary exactly because the Court has no power base of its own. A third reason for the failure, if I may say so, was a judicial arrogance that refused to believe that the public should be told the truth instead of being fed on slogans and platitudes. The fourth problem is even less soluble. It is that many of the Justices were incapable of doing better. They fooled not only the public but themselves.

There is need for intelligence and integrity on the bench that goes far beyond an average I.Q. and a distaste for venality. The Court, in performing what is, by definition, an unpopular task, is none the less dependent on popular support to keep it a viable institution.

If the Court's primary substantive function is impaired by these defects, so too is its important symbolic office:

A gentle and generous philosopher noted the other day a growing "intuition" on the part of the masses that all judges, in lively controversies, are "more or less prejudiced." But between the "more or less" lies the whole kingdom of the mind, the difference between the "more or less" are the triumphs of disinterestedness, they are the aspirations we call justice . . . The basic considerations in the vitality of any system of law is con-

fidence in this proximate purity of its process. Corruption from venality is hardly
more damaging than a widespread belief
of corrosion through partisanship. Our
judicial system is absolutely dependent
upon a popular belief that it is as untainted
in its workings as the finite limitations of
disciplined human minds and feelings
make possible.

And here again the Warren Court has
failed us. What Arthur Schlesinger has
termed a crisis of confidence clearly extends to the Supreme Court. The restoration of that confidence is vital to the
continuance of the rule of law in this
country. For above everything else, the
Supreme Court is symbolic of America's
preference for law over force as the
ruling mechanism in a democratic society. If it fails, the vital center disappears, and we "must ultimately decay
either from anarchy, or from the slow
atrophy of a life stifled by useless
shadows."

The Nixon Court has awesome tasks
before it. To match the Warren Court
aspirations for the protection of individuals and minorities that today justifies the Court's existence. To restore
the confidence of the American public
in the rule of law. One or the other is
not enough.

These essays of judicial activism and judicial restraint should, of course, be read in conjunction with the relevant case material. The classic series of cases ought to be consulted: economic powers, civil rights, rights of persons accused of crimes, free speech and assembly, separation of church and state, reapportionment, and the incorporation of the due process clause of the Fourteenth Amendment. The authors of the selections found in this volume are storehouses of additional material. Many of their works are cited at the beginning of each selection.

Beyond that, the following discussions of both judicial activism and judicial restraint would be useful: Harold J. Spaeth, *The Warren Court* (Chandler, 1966); Robert J. Steamer, "Statesmanship or Craftsmanship: Current Conflict over the Supreme Court," 11 *Western Political Quarterly* 265 (1968); Henry J. Schmandt, *Courts in the American Political System* (Dickenson, 1968); Henry J. Abraham, *The Judiciary* (Oxford, 1968); Walter F. Murphy and C. Herman Pritchett, *Courts, Judges, and Politics* (Random House, 1961); Charles S. Hyneman, *The Supreme Court on Trial* (Atherton, 1963); Eugene V. Rostow, *The Sovereign Prerogative* (Yale University Press, 1962); Edward McWhinney, "The Great Debate: Activism and Self-restraint and Current Dilemmas in Judicial Policy-Making," 33 *New York University Law Quarterly* 775 (1958); J. G. Deutsch, "Neutrality, Legitimacy, and the Supreme Court: Some Intersections between Law and Political Science," 20 *Stanford Law Review* 169 (1968); M. D. Forkosch, "Separation of Powers," 41 *University of Colorado Law Review* 529 (1969); Herbert Jacob, *Justice in America*, (Little Brown, 1965); Carl Brent Swisher, *The Supreme Court in Modern Role* (New York University Press, 1965).

One may discover fine analyses of the restraintist position in Phil C. Neal, "Baker v. Carr: Politics in Search of Law" in Kurland, *The Supreme Court and the Constitution* (University of Chicago Press, 1965); George D. Braden, "The Search for Objectivity in Constitutional Law," 57 *Yale Law Journal* 571 (1948); Henry Steele Commager, *Majority Rule and Minority Rights* (Oxford, 1943); James B. Thayer, "The Origin and Scope of the American Doctrine of Constitutional Law," 7 *Harvard Law Review* 129 (1893); Marian Irish, "Mr. Justice Douglas and Judicial Restraint," 6 *University of Florida Law Review* 537 (1953); Robert S. Lancaster, "Judge Learned Hand and the Limits of Judicial Discretion," 9 *Vanderbilt Law Review* 427 (1956); Philip B. Kurland, "Equal in Origin and Title to the Legislative and Executive Branches of Government," 78 *Harvard Law Review* 143 (1964); Potter Stewart and John Marshall Harlan, "Robert H. Jackson's Influence on Federal-State Relationships," 23 *The Record* 7 (1968); J. D. Noland, "Stare Decisis and the Overruling of Constitutional Decisions in the Warren Years," 4 *Valparaiso University Law Review* 101 (1969); C. B. Blackmar, "The Supreme Court as a Governmental Institution," 12 *St. Louis University Law Journal* 237 (1967); Bernard Goodwin, "The Supreme Court: Viable Fallibilism or Fatal Infallibility," 23 *Vanderbilt Law Review* 251 (1970); Alexander Bickel, "The New Supreme Court: Prospects and Problems," 45 *Tulane Law Review* 229 (1971); Paul C. Bartholomew, "Our 'Legislative' Courts," 46 *Southwestern Social Science Quarterly* 11 (1965).

Most works concerned with the issue of judicial review carry with them a direct or indirect implication defending the phenomenon of judicial activism. The most prolific defenders of an activist court are those authors whose selections appeared in this volume. A few other examples include Robert A. Dahl, "Decision-making in a Democracy: the Supreme Court as a National Policy-Maker," 6 *Journal of Public Law* No. 2 (1957); Joseph F. Menz, "A Brief in Support of the Supreme Court," 54

Northwestern University Law Review 30 (1959); William O. Douglas, *The Right of the People* (Doubleday, 1958); Arthur A. North, S.J., *The Supreme Court: Judicial Process and Judicial Politics* (Appleton-Century-Crofts, 1964); J. H. Choper, "On the Warren Court and Judicial Review," 17 *Catholic University Law Review* 20 (1967); W. F. Swindler, "The Warren Court: Completion of a Constitutional Revolution," 23 *Vanderbilt Law Review* 205 (1970).